T0386420

An Introduction to Grounded Methodology for Emerging Educational Researchers

Introducing the reader to grounded methodology and its ethical approach, this book explores the theory behind the method as well as how to use it to develop and evaluate learning and education projects.

Grounded methodology is designed to challenge traditional educational research methodologies, and in doing so questions the notion of the need for highly formal research in institutional settings. In this respect, it is also a simple way of planning an educational project that needs an evaluative element. Covering data collection techniques used in the course of education research such as observations, interviews, course development, participant diaries and online data collection, this book investigates the practical realities of researching in education contexts and the differences in educational, national and cultural backgrounds.

It is ideal reading for students and academics looking to update and increase their knowledge on grounded methodology, especially students who are researchers in final-year undergraduate or postgraduate level programs, or instructors planning to teach grounded theory or grounded methodology to their own emerging research students.

Simon Hayhoe is a Reader in Education at the University of Bath, UK. He is also a Centre Associate in the Centre for the Philosophy of Natural and Social Science, London School of Economics, an Associate of the Scottish Sensory Centre, University of Edinburgh and Temporary Advisor to the World Health Organisation. Simon's current work focuses on qualitative and visual methodologies, visual impairment and education, disability arts, access to cultural heritage and accessible and inclusive technology.

Qualitative and Visual Methodologies in Educational Research

Series Editors: Rita Chawla-Duggan and Simon Hayhoe

University of Bath, UK

We are increasingly living in an era where students and researchers are under severe time pressures, whilst the amount of research topics, methodologies, data collection methods and ethical questions continue to grow. The *Qualitative and Visual Methodologies in Educational Research* series provides concise, accessible texts that take account of the methodological issues that emerge out of researching educational issues. They are ideal reading for all those designing and implementing unfamiliar qualitative research methods, from undergraduates to the most experienced researchers.

Books in the series:

- Are compact, comprehensive works, to appeal to final year undergraduates and early career postgraduates, at masters and doctoral level – both PhD and EdD. These works can also be easily read and digested by emerging, early career researchers, or raise issues applicable to experienced researchers who are keeping up with their field.
- Reflect on a single methodological problem per volume. In particular, the titles examine data analysis, research design, access, sampling, ethics, the role of theory, and how fieldwork is experienced in real-time.
- Have chapters that discuss the context of education, teaching and learning, and so can include a psychological as well as social and cultural understanding of teaching and learning in non-traditional or non-formal, as well as formal settings.
- Include discussions that engage critically with ontological and epistemological debates underpinning the choice of qualitative or visual methodologies in educational research.

The *Qualitative and Visual Methodologies in Educational Research* series includes books which stimulate ideas and help the reader design important and insightful research that improves the lives of others though education, to ultimately inspire the development of qualitative and visual methodologies.

Titles in the series include:

An Introduction to Grounded Methodology for Emerging Educational Researchers
Simon Hayhoe

An Introduction to Grounded Methodology for Emerging Educational Researchers

Simon Hayhoe

Routledge
Taylor & Francis Group

LONDON AND NEW YORK

First published 2021
by Routledge
2 Park Square, Milton Park, Abingdon, Oxon OX14 4RN

and by Routledge
52 Vanderbilt Avenue, New York, NY 10017

Routledge is an imprint of the Taylor & Francis Group, an informa business

British Library Cataloguing-in-Publication Data
A catalogue record for this book is available from the British Library

Library of Congress Cataloging-in-Publication Data
Names: Hayhoe, Simon, author.
Title: An introduction to grounded methodology for emerging educational
    researchers / Simon Hayhoe.
Description: Abingdon, Oxon ; New York, NY : Routledge, 2021. | Series:
    Qualitative and visual methodologies in educational research | Includes
    bibliographical references and index.
Identifiers: LCCN 2020019394 (print) | LCCN 2020019395 (ebook) |
    ISBN 9780367426811 (hardback) | ISBN 9780367854393 (ebook)
Subjects: LCSH: Education—Research—Methodology. | Education—Data
    processing.
Classification: LCC LB1028 .H365 2020 (print) | LCC LB1028 (ebook) |
    DDC 370.21—dc23
LC record available at https://lccn.loc.gov/2020019394
LC ebook record available at https://lccn.loc.gov/2020019395

ISBN: 978-0-367-42681-1 (hbk)
ISBN: 978-0-367-85439-3 (ebk)

Typeset in Times New Roman
by Apex CoVantage, LLC

Contents

Contributors

Helena Garcia Carrizosa is a Research Associate and PhD student at the Open University. From October 2016 to January 2020, she was a partner of the European Commission's ARCHES project. Prior to working for the Open University, she studied at the Courtauld Institute of Art and University College London and worked for the National Portrait Gallery.

Jonathan Rix is Professor of Learning Support at the Open University. His research interests focus upon creating policies, practices and language that facilitate inclusion within the mainstream; capturing diverse perspectives; and developing models to facilitate our thinking about the form and function of education. Professor Rix has a strong and broad interest in issues relating to learning difficulties and issues of equality and participation.

Jane Seale is Professor of Education at the Open University. She has developed a national and international profile in the field through key roles such as President of the Association for Learning Technology (2006–2007) and Digital Inclusion consultant to the Economic and Social Research Council (ESRC)-funded Technology Enhanced Learning (TEL) Programme in the UK (2009–2012). Between 2007 and 2010, Professor Seale was Co-Director of the ESRC National Centre for Research Methods. She has recently served on the REF 2014 Education panel in the UK, which had the responsibility for assessing the quality of research conducted in UK universities.

Kieron Sheehy is Professor of Education (innovation pedagogies) at the Open University. His research interests are within the broad field of inclusive education, often focusing on how teaching approaches or services can be developed to successfully support diverse groups of learners. Professor Sheehy supervises research within this area and has an interest in addressing issues for those who might be stigmatised and excluded within educational systems.

Series editor introduction

We are increasingly living in an era where students and researchers are under severe time pressures. At the same time, research topics, methodologies, data collection methods and the ethical questions we face are constantly growing. In 2018, this dilemma was the impetus for the book series. As book editors, we were conscious of the fact there are very few short, manageable methodology texts available to inform our intellectual choices. And yet, whilst we wanted to address this gap, we did not want to compromise the quality of the material, discussion or the evidence that students and researchers could draw upon.

Consequently, in outlining our ideas for the book series, we decided to involve writers who could both theorise methodological problems and who were also in the field of practice, experiencing the pressures, dilemmas and uncertainty of real face-to-face research. This series therefore includes accounts of methodological issues that emerge out of researching educational issues, that even the most experienced researchers face in designing and implementing their project proposals.

As our ideas for the book series evolved, we realised that our own students and early-career colleagues were producing innovative research designs. In addition, these students and colleagues were addressing difficult methodological problems in both local and global contexts, in some of the most sophisticated ways imaginable. Consequently, our intention for this book series was to go beyond the experienced social science researcher interested in the study of education, to include a student and emerging professional authorship and readership.

The books in the series:

- Are compact, intense works, to appeal to final-year undergraduates and early-career postgraduates, at masters and doctoral level – both PhD and EdD. These works can also be easily read and digested by emerging, early-career researchers, or raise issues applicable to experienced researchers who are keeping up with their field.

- Reflect on a single methodological problem per volume. In particular, the titles examine data analysis, research design, access, sampling, ethics, the role of theory and how fieldwork is experienced in real time.
- Have chapters that discuss the context of education, teaching and learning, and so can include a psychological as well as social and cultural understanding of teaching and learning in non-traditional or non-formal, as well as formal, settings.
- Include discussions that engage critically with ontological and epistemological debates underpinning the choice of qualitative or visual methodologies in educational research.

The series *Qualitative and Visual Methodologies in Educational Research* is not designed solely for educationalists. Our authors are from several disciplinary fields and their theories, topics and settings are not tied to a single geographical or cultural region or background. Their contextual focus, however, remains always concerned with education. Thus, our disciplinary authorship and readership includes, for example, people interested in the sociology of education, educational technology, educational psychology, educational inclusion, international education, education in developing countries and early childhood and primary education.

Finally, when designing our book series, we wanted to include books that we would like to see in our own research methods courses, but we also wanted to include and encourage authors to discuss theories that we ourselves would want to read about. Both of us teach and are experienced in developing research methods courses, yet at the same time we hold responsibilities that help us appreciate the needs of different educational communities: for example, one of us is the Director of Studies for MPhil and PhD students and teaches Masters-level Research Methods units via blended learning, whilst the other is the unit coordinator for MA and MRes methodology units, and teaches on EdD-level units during summer schools. Furthermore, both of us are highly experienced researchers, each with over twenty years' experience in the field, and yet we are still learning, still fighting to keep up to date, still trying to innovate through our own fieldwork and writing. This work is challenging and exhausting, but it is always an exciting and creative enterprise.

With this in mind, we hope you enjoy reading the books in the series as much as we enjoy commissioning them. If they stimulate ideas, and help you design important and insightful research that improves the lives of others though education, then we will have shown the value of collective innovation through research. Most importantly, through engaging with this series, be inspired to develop your own qualitative and visual methodologies, become leaders in your own fields and inspire others to innovate new forms of research, education and learning.

Rita Chawla-Duggan and Simon Hayhoe
Series Editors, University of Bath, UK

1 Introduction

This book examines the philosophy, principles and most importantly the practice of grounded methodology. It also examines the ethics of grounded methodology's design and theory and introduces the reader to the practical use of grounded methodology through case studies of related projects. In addition, this book addresses the following hypothesis about grounded methodology:

> Grounded methodology focuses on the theory that relationships can most often provide the richest understanding of our human societies and cultures. These relationships are, most importantly, the relationships formed between people, communities, institutions, epistemologies (that is families or types of knowledge) or forms of learning. However, in addition to "real world" relationships, grounded methodology also focuses on relationships between data, categories of data and the underlying relationships that underpin similarities or differences between these data and categories.

In doing so, the book features the application of grounded methodology through data collection methodologies used in the course of educational research using grounded methodology. These data collection methods include observations, interviews, the development of educational projects and systematic practitioner reflection, and systematic literature searches and online data collection methods.

The case studies and data collection methods in this book are projects I've designed, and this should be born in mind whilst reading them. For, although this book uses examples of research on disability, these are merely illustrative of the research methodology used in these studies and the implementation of a model of practice and analysis. The focus of this book is always the design and use of grounded methodology in educational contexts, how it came into being and how it is now used in research and teaching studies.

Consequently, when you finish reading this book, you should understand the process of grounded methodology as well as its theoretical background. You should also understand how this methodology can develop your understanding of educational contexts and practice, as well as its institutions and policies.

This book's primary aims are to: 1) *introduce* a grounded methodology approach through an exploration of its framework amongst existing models; 2) *argue* that the study of educational institutions has too often focused on the idea that there can only be a single understanding of institutions through common experience; and 3) *investigate* the practical realities of researching educational institutions and differences in educational identities. Similarly, this book's primary objectives are to: 1) equip readers to *develop* critical analyses of traditional studies of educational institutions using social and cultural models from parallel disciplines; 2) equip its readers with the ability to *deconstruct* traditional methods of data collection and analysis to develop a multi-layered philosophical approach to educational research; and 3) *introduce* a framework of an essentially more ethical research and an epistemological approach to studying educational institutions.

As the title of this book suggests, I have written this text with emergent researchers in mind. Emergent researchers can be undergraduate students negotiating their first dissertations or extended projects to gain honours, or postgraduate students studying research methods or writing their first masters or doctoral dissertations. Emergent researchers can also be those doing their first professional research project for work, or perhaps those who are already social researchers but are considering using grounded methodology for the first time.

Finally, this book is also designed for those planning to teach grounded theory or grounded methodology to their own emerging research students.

So, what makes this book different?

Hopefully, you are picking up this book having heard about grounded theory, even though you may be curious as to the difference between grounded theory and grounded methodology – or you may be asking yourself: is there one? You may also have read something about grounded theory from the many excellent monographs or chapters in edited books on social science and want to know how you can apply it to your educational research project. This is where this book is different.

Although many books include an analysis of grounded theory in education, these often do not present a single framework or description of data collection methods in relation to studies of institutions. Fewer books relate specifically to education, the study of practicing education or use alternative methods of data collection, such as the Web or academic databases. And, of these books, fewer still examine fieldwork, case studies or pure systematic literature reviews using this grounded approach, or chart such research projects from beginning to end.

This is hopefully what makes this book of greater help to you than traditional, simpler theoretical discussions.

Second, by reading this book you are walking in the footsteps of successful, sometimes award-winning research in this field. Many of the studies and the data analysis in the following chapters have already formed the basis of peer-reviewed and internationally recognised studies; many of these studies have received substantial funding; and all of these studies have been peer-reviewed. The methods and the fieldwork discussed in this book are therefore a subject of international work, and they have been tested for their significance in many educational contexts. The majority of these studies have also had direct impact on policy and practice in the field.

The structure of this book

The book contains six chapters including this introduction, which are set out as follows:

Chapter 2: From Grounded Theory to Grounded Methodology. This chapter analyses the early theories of researching through grounded theory, focuses on issues with grounded theory analysis, introduces the theory of grounded methodology and discusses how conducting grounded methodology studies in institutional settings is different. Importantly, it introduces the key issue related to this methodology, which is the use of relationships in education. Most importantly, this is the study of relationships among people within communities, and secondarily this is the study of relationships between datum and categories of data.

Chapter 3: Grounded Methodology and Field Research. This chapter discusses a study which used grounded methodology to analyse pilot tests and evaluate participatory practice. The aim of the study was to help develop and evaluate inclusive technologies for a large, multi-country project called Accessible Resources for Cultural Heritage Eco-Systems (ARCHES). The analysis for this evaluation was conducted using grounded methodology in a traditional way, and included interviews and structured exercises as data collection methods. Its outcomes fed into the design of educational technologies and key performance indicators that were designed to inform the policies of the European Union, which funded the study.

Chapter 4: Grounded Methodology and Developing Education. This chapter discusses a study using grounded methodology in a non-traditional way, to develop an arts education project. This project was designed to teach the community in the city of Bath about the history and dangers of flooding. The aim of the project was to commission artworks which were accessible to marginalised groups and to develop a system of using them for teaching and evaluating the process of development. This study included reflection, project design and management, the employment of a new methodology of inclusion, observations of the implementation of artworks, visual methods, exhibitions and interviews.

Chapter 5: Grounded Methodology and Systematic Literature Reviews. This chapter discusses another study using grounded methodology in a non-traditional way, this time to conduct a systematic literature review on mobile technologies and learners with visual impairments. The aim of the study was to examine the nature of inclusion and technology for learners with visual impairments, to understand how other academics theorised inclusion and the use of technologies, and to research the difference between educators and engineers in this regard. Subsequently, the study included a survey of the trade press and institutional literature as well as academic literature.

Chapter 6: Conclusion. This chapter includes a summary of the findings of the previous chapters.

2 From grounded theory to grounded methodology

Introduction

This chapter provides an overview of the foundation of grounded theory and then grounded methodology. In providing this overview, I show how the latter evolved from the former. More particularly, this chapter shows the philosophy that underpins these methodologies and their construction; how grounded theory was created and the era that created it; and why I felt that grounded methodology should be a new, more distinct methodology.

Significantly, this chapter is framed by two simple messages, which can also be applied to the case studies and data analysis throughout the book.

The first message repeats the hypothesis in Chapter 1 and emphasises that grounded methodology is focused on relationships. This is to say, these studies are about relationships between data; they are about relationships among themes, categories, variables and case studies; they are about the distance that separates these relationships; and they are about underpinning relationships. Most importantly, grounded methodology is first and foremost about human social and cultural relationships. It is about how people are connected or are different, or in other words, what makes people and communities *who they are* in comparison to others.

The second message is that, like grounded theory, grounded methodology is mostly interested in social or cultural processes when used in the study of education. These processes can include practice, policy development, learning, movement or technology usage, to name but a few. This second message has resonance with me, as I originally trained in a college of art and design, where we talked about performance and product. That is to say, the drawing (the product) is the creation of how we made the drawing (the process). In grounded methodology, our data collection and analysis strategies and techniques are all about the process, with the product of education merely being an illustration of what we have ended up with.

Three important definitions used in this chapter

Before beginning this chapter, it is important to define one word and two phrases in relation to the study of methodology. The word I need to define is *hypothesis*, which is a statement that can be tested with data as evidence, such as "the earth is round" or "the earth is flat." In a very particular way, the hypothesis in science and social science is the catalyst of any study, much like a research question.

The two phrases I need to define are *inductive logic* and *deductive logic*. These two phrases represent huge areas of study that have been considered since Athenian philosophers such as the Sophists. However, in science and social science, they have a specific relationship to theory and hypothesis testing, and as I will show later, they are central to our understanding of grounded theory and grounded methodology.

Put simply, inductive logic in science and social science is the philosophical belief that we can only create a theory about something after data about it is collected. This also often insinuates that when interpreting these forms of study that, if something cannot be observed, it cannot be understood as "real." For instance, if we were to study millions of people's diets to find out what causes cancer and discover those who drink red wine and olive oil are much less likely to have cancer, then we can hypothesise that these foods can decrease the risk of cancer. Therefore, the ideas that drinking olive oil and red wine reduces the risk of cancer has been induced through study.

With similar simplicity, deductive logic can be said to be the belief that we can deduce reality initially through logical argument, reasoning and discussion before testing it. To put it another way, I have hypothesised at the beginning of this book that: "Relationships can most often provide the richest understanding of our human societies and cultures." This hypothesis is based on my experience and therefore could be said to be unproven and therefore deductive.

There are two important aspects to this form of deductive logic that are important to know when studying any form of methodology: 1) they are often reliant on a passage of time to prove a hypothesis through study, and this passage of time can affect the nature of your data, the type of data you collect, the reliability of your data and even your hypothesis; 2) if you are a positivist, then you believe in deductive logic as a form of historicism; this is the belief that there are rules to history and things will happen in the future just because they've also happened in the past (Popper, 1999).

For example, a pharmacologist might deduce that a drug might work on a form of disease because it has worked on a similar disease in the past. The pharmacologist might then conduct a drugs trial over a fixed number of years to see if this hypothesis is true. Predictive models such as economic or weather forecasts can also be said to use deductive logic, although they are not scientific. It is only when a predicted passage of time has finished, and a model's predictions can be tested, that they can be said to be scientific. Thus, predictive models are merely deductive hypotheses before this future evidence can be collected to test the model.

The aims of this chapter

This chapter has two aims. The first aim is to provide you with an informed choice of where and when it is best and most appropriate to use grounded theory or grounded methodology. It also points you to reasons as to why you should not use either methodology if they are not needed, if your study warrants a combination of methodologies or either methodology is inappropriate.

The second aim is to allow you to consider the *nature* of methodology, an issue that is frequently considered by experienced researchers, and one that is increasingly important for emerging researchers to consider. It also aims to allow you to consider why we need a methodology at all, or if we do need a methodology, does it matter what it is? This again is a perennial consideration by research students, as I would argue that it is always important to consider what is the purpose of having a blueprint, a philosophy or a function for your research.

To begin to address these aims, this chapter is broken into the following sections: 1) The early history of grounded theory – this section explains the context of grounded theory, how it was created and its intellectual underpinnings; 2) The principles of grounded theory – this section examines the fundamental components of grounded theory; 3) The development of grounded methodology – in this section, I discuss grounded methodology, its unique elements and how it works; and 4) the Conclusion – lastly, I summarise the observations made in this chapter.

The early history of grounded theory

There are two concepts that you need to understand as we study the history of methodology. First, when I introduce the principles of methodology to research students at Bath, I always ask them, "Who came up with the idea of methodology in the first place, and are the methodologies that we use today a *natural* way of looking at society?" This not only leads to heated discussions, but it also gets to the roots of what a methodology is, as we never come up with a single, coherent, agreed-upon answer.

This is the point about methodology. There is not just a single answer or belief to methodology, and there is also no single, perfect way to study all things in all contexts and in all environments. Thus, social science will never stand still. Through the development and evolution of methodology, the progress of a methodology is never ending and forever expanding and hopefully improving. And, it is only through this expansion and improvement that social science will get better.

I argue that studying the history of grounded theory is a good example of looking at expansion and hopefully improvement, as it represents a perfect example of the fecundity and different opinions that form methodologies. Moreover, through studying this development of grounded theory, whose evolution is modern and can be traced back to only a few academics, we can observe a powerful example to teach or write about the fragility of the design of methodology.

Second, there are two distinct poles of opinion on the issue of our need for methodology: 1) those who believe that we need highly structured, reproducible methodologies to grasp what they believe is *an objective* truth (Lakatos, 2015); and 2) those who believe that we will never find *the* truth, only *a* truth, and so one methodology is as good as another (Motterlini, 1999; Feyerabend, 1993).

Everyone in social and cultural research can be said to be in between these poles, as there is no easy answer to this issue, and you must find your own way through experience in your field. However, whatever your position on methodology or your philosophical belief, the *simple* truth is if you want to get a paper published, a conference abstract accepted or your assignment graded, you will have to discuss methodology.

So, how does methodology evolve? Well, in the case of grounded theory, by crisis, by a need for a break with tradition and by individual arguments among researchers.

The methodological context of grounded theory

To understand the evolution of grounded theory fully, it is also important to briefly understand the epistemological landscape of social and cultural theorisation and methodology at the birth of grounded theory in the 1950s and 1960s (Hayhoe, 2012). Prior to the "discovery" of this methodology, social and cultural research largely resembled a miasma of studies, approaches and philosophies. These studies, approaches and philosophies could be said to be guided by a general principle, the principle that communities and societies had unifying and underpinning qualities or a single underpinning quality. However, the "discovery" of grounded theory also happened in the era of at least three significant upheavals of methodology that contributed to a disturbance in our understanding of social and cultural qualities.

First, sociological studies were said to be undergoing *a crisis* in this era (Deflem, 2013), one in which grand theories were felt to be increasingly conservative and authoritarian, despite their left-leaning or liberal rhetoric. At this point sociology was relying on large studies, such as *The Authoritarian Personality*, first published in 1950 (Adorno et al., 2019). This study attempted to adjudge human personality traits according to largely political scales including, controversially, an "F Scale," which tried to predict personalities pertaining to fascism – itself, an arguably totalitarian notion. Similarly, published in the 1960s, *Towards a General Theory of Action* (Parsons et al., 1965) attempted to construct a grand theory of human activity that could be applied to all societies and adopted as a framework for studying universal behaviours.

Second, during the 1950s and 1960s, the subject of anthropology, which was traditionally considered to be a branch of the natural sciences, was increasingly looking at the differences between human communities via purely social or cultural data. Consequently, anthropology was increasingly seen as a branch of the humanities, one that traded in highly localised studies with largely narrative literature. For instance, in Britain influential authors such as Evans-Pritchard (1962) were popularising social anthropology as a subject, with a methodology largely based on participant observation. Similarly, in North America writers such as Goffman (1959) and Geertz (1989) took anthropology further into the realms of the social sciences and legitimised more structured analyses. This led to modes of approaching data through "thick description," which could be applied to issues of cultural eccentricities, such as attitudes toward gender or a belief in common sense (Geertz, 1989).

Third, in the late 1950s and early 1960s, English language philosophies were casting doubt on positivism and the objectivity of scientific methodology, particularly questioning the subjective nature of data, evidence and proof. The foundation of this philosophy was Popper's (1934) criticism of traditional notions of induction and deduction in science. These philosophies were the cornerstones of debates on positivism and the belief that the truth can only be determined through observations and direct experience of "reality."

By contrast, writing originally in German, Popper proposed a theory of Critical Rationalism and falsifiability, the philosophy that science can only prove, not disprove, and that nature has no laws or underlying logic. This theory was first published in English in 1959 (Popper, 1959), and was followed by further work on falsification by Popper (1963) and his former student Lakatos (1970) in the 1960s. In this era, both writers were working out of the London School of Economics and, more particularly, Popper's Centre for the Philosophy of Natural and Social Science.

Popper's disparagement of positivism would subsequently lead to a more specific criticism of scientific theory generation through notions of the fallibility of objective theory in the UK and more importantly in the US. In this decade, such criticism propagated a growing belief in a form of scientific tribalism generating illogical, biased or traditional academic paradigms and cultures of theory that could only change through revolutions of thought (Kuhn, 1962).

The "discovery" of grounded theory

Glaser and Strauss were the first to develop grounded theory in the early 1960s – or as they claimed at the time, "discovered" it – to conduct a sociological study of an awareness of dying (Glaser & Strauss, 1965). It can be said that in this era of upheaval of social and cultural theory, the early development of this methodology thus became a reflection of these changes in social science, and one that reflected its turmoil. The topic of its first study also reflected this upheaval, centred as it was on patients and carers in a hospital in the San Francisco Bay Area of Northern California and aimed to examine the understanding of controversial aspects of mortality.

Glaser and Strauss' study was problematic from the start. The issues encountered were unique, and the issue of an awareness of dying was under-researched, meaning that there was no frame of reference, no precise literature and no theory or hypothecation they could refer to. Furthermore, Glaser and Strauss did not know the participants they would meet, they had no pre-arranged system of sampling, they did not know if communities of patients existed and they did not know what variables bound them together. Importantly, what they were trying to investigate was intangible, and therefore difficult to measure and observe, which would add an extra layer of complexity to their field research.

Consequently, Glaser and Strauss had to find a new model of sociological research practice that would provide them with an understanding of the intangible concept of "awareness" and "dying." This would have to be a methodology that could make the best of the close observation of anthropological techniques and strive for the objectivity of what sociology purported to be at the time. Furthermore, what they would have to come to terms with was that the data they hoped to collect and analyse was largely descriptive, and the population they were studying was relatively small. Thus, turning this data into numbers would be difficult and reduce its meaning.

These problems were particularly difficult for both to justify against their research training, as the methodological tradition of American sociologists was largely centred on quantitative data. Perhaps significantly for Glaser (1998), he had been taught by Paul Lazarsfeld, who was known as the father of empirical sociology in the US (Jeřábek, 2001). This led them to develop strategies on which grounded theory was developed.

The principles of grounded theory

In *The Discovery of Grounded Theory*, Glaser and Strauss (1967) described strategies that would take largely qualitative data that they could describe as generating theory. N.B. In real-life studies, quantitative data is also used to a lesser extent during analysis, although the principle method of gathering and analysing this data was through a comparison of its qualities. In the research studies that followed, these strategies could be broadly interpreted as principles that underpinned doing a grounded theory study.

The first and perhaps most important of these principles was that data should be generated using inductive logic. Given the context of this era, it is arguable that the philosophy of grounded theory in its earliest years faced two problems in trying to be a purely inductive methodology. First, the methodology was arguably searching for a solution to the crisis in sociology by trying to reject subjective notions and personal bias, such as that shown by writers such as Adorno. Second, the methodology was trying to find a way to produce induction from abstract data that did not lend itself to observation in the way that social anthropology was capturing – i.e. abstract beliefs about dying and mortality. Thus, it was not possible to reliably watch and count practice or behaviour or develop unnatural experiments where variables could be automatically controlled. Subsequently, observable patterns between the data had to become part of this inductive process.

The second principle was "All is Data," which is to say all data that can be collected should be collected, and that all this data needs to be collected and analysed simultaneously and compared with all data that has already been collected. This latter facet of grounded theory was otherwise known as "Constant Comparison." In order to develop observable patterns and relationships between concepts and categories of concepts, grounded theory needed to have vast amounts of data, certainly far more than similar studies using other methodologies. Thus, grounded theory studies generally emphasised field-based studies. Furthermore, unlike many other studies that researchers were used to at the time, academic literature could also be thought of as data itself, thus reading research literature was thought to be a form of data collection.

The third principle was the constant memoing of data that was produced as a direct consequence of Constant Comparison. These memos were generated by constantly making short, reflexive, impressionistic notes on paper or card. During memoing, relationships and categories were defined, and links were made between and within categories. Consequently, whilst looking at data that had been observed, a note was made of how this data fit other data that had already been collected, how this data related to other data that had been gathered and the categories and sub-categories that this data related to. One other use of memoing was that it allowed concepts and categories of data that did not fit the study to be rejected or kept for later studies. In the modern era, these patterns and relationships are created, and memos generated digitally through qualitative analysis software such as NVivo.

The fourth principle that emerged from grounded theory was that studies should be conducted in three distinct phases of investigation; these were termed the Open, Axial and Selective Coding Phases. During Open Coding, the researcher was said to enter the field from a naïve perspective, collecting and analysing data without any assumptions about or knowledge of the topic being studied. During this phase, researchers look for initial patterns in their data that can be taken forward into the Axial Phase.

During the Axial Phase, these categories are probed further with new data, often from different participant populations, to further develop and validate the categories, sub-categories and their relationships. Following this new phase of comparison, a tentative hypothesis is developed that can be tested. The purpose of the Selective Phase, therefore, is to test this tentative hypothesis with new data, or if this is not possible, existing data can be re-analysed in a different way. Thus, the project finishes with a testing and improvement of the hypothesis.

However, differing from the course of traditional research in this era, the final testing of the hypothesis was not an end point in the research. Grounded theories were developed to become the starting, middle and end points of larger studies. Grounded theory methodology thus trained its authors and technicians to become specialists and experts in their fields and sought to encourage the study of topics that had rarely, if ever, been studied. I must admit, as a researcher who was originally studying the arts education of visually impaired students using ethnomethodology, this latter aspect of grounded theory particularly appealed to me.

The development of grounded methodology

More than two decades after the "discovery" of grounded theory, a theoretical split occurred between Glaser and Strauss. Although later described as dramatic, the causes of this theoretical split are not relevant to this book, and they are reportedly so complex that they could be the subject of a study itself. However, what is important to understand from this split is what happened to Glaser and Strauss afterward.

Even as I write, Glaser (1998, 2001) maintains what can be described as an orthodox stance on grounded theory. By contrast, in the late 1980s and early 1990s, Strauss joined the nursing theorist Juliet Corbin to form what can be described as a less positivist understanding of the methodology (Strauss & Corbin, 1990). This evolution occurred further into the new millennium, when writers such as Kathy Charmaz (2006) discussed socially and arguably culturally constructivist interpretations of grounded theory for its use in generating theory.

So, what is grounded methodology and why is it different?

To address the first part of this question, it is first necessary to explain the name *grounded methodology*. This name was chosen because when I developed this methodology, I wanted to emphasise that the methodology would ground my research, just as it does with grounded theory. However, I also wanted this methodology to distance itself from the philosophy that the theory I was developing was in some way generating or inducing theories spontaneously and uncreatively (Hayhoe, 2012). More on this later.

In developing this new methodology from grounded theory, but remaining theoretically distinct from it, I also wanted to emphasise that grounded methodology still retains three principles of grounded theory. I found these principles practically and theoretically useful for conducting fieldwork or analysis and related to its ways of conducting research.

The first principle I kept was the three phases of coding, and in many of my following studies I have often continued to call these the Open, Axial and Selective Phases out of tradition. These names are also useful, as many readers can relate to these phase names as part of a general grounded study. These three phases are particularly useful as they logically triangulate the findings of regular field studies and allow the development of research, education or design projects in manageable stages.

For example, when collecting data during a field study, I can concentrate on three different population samples during each of the three phases or use different forms of data collection method, such as interviewing or observation, per phase. In addition, I can also use the three different methods of analysis of grounded theory to triangulate the data in its different forms.

The second principle I kept was the need to create a central hypothesis from any form of data I could gather. As with grounded theory, it was decided that grounded methodology would continue to compare data, refine its methodology and regard all forms of data collected during the project as equally important, valuable and useable. However, as part of this comparison of data, for clarity of output it was also decided to focus on creating relationships and categories of issues, practices, policies, literature, epistemology and so forth. This arguably cleaner and more flexible approach to data collection suited the reflexive, problem-solving approaches to new contexts, topics and settings. It also allowed me to develop studies with highly practical aims, such as the development of technologies or specific education projects, and apply for research projects with defined aims, questions and set periods of time.

The third principle I kept was the specialist nature of grounded studies and the way in which one study led onto another study, to evolve and improve my own knowledge as a researcher. This was perhaps the most powerful principle for me as a practitioner-researcher (I was a schoolteacher when I worked on my first grounded methodology study) who was wedded to my research topic rather than my academic career at the time.

As time has passed, however, the development of new studies whilst becoming a full-time academic became advantageous as it allowed me to develop my own research narrative of study and practice. Although branching off occasionally to look at sub-topics of sensory disability and education, the continual nature of grounded methodology studies mostly allowed me to build a portfolio of co-ordinated research and literature.

***

Although retaining elements of grounded theory in grounded methodology, there were of course issues with grounded theory that made me want to create a space between the two forms of methodology. The first of these issues was central to the formation of a different type of methodology. The other issue was related to its practical application.

First, the central problem I found with grounded theory was that it was specifically designed in the belief that data induced testable theories. By rejecting this notion, I found that grounded methodology studies could acknowledge the social and cultural construction of its study more, and I could start studies with small hypotheses and research questions. This process also increased the chances of raising funding and being acceptable by exam boards and ethics committees, which often required hypotheses and questions in their proposals.

This does not mean that grounded methodology studies should not create testable theories, or that they do not need evidence to inform their theories. To simply believe in a string of deductive ideas without any need for evidence would be unscientific. However, one of the main issues with grounded theory even in this modern era is its slavish adherence to inductive logic, and the issue that the data it produces can demarcate coherent patterns and categories and refute weak ones.

In the past, the belief in pure induction most importantly led grounded theory to defend another of its controversial beliefs, that is, the belief that researchers must enter field studies from a completely naïve perspective (Glaser & Strauss, 1967). This belief promoted the practice of starting a research project without any knowledge of the field you are about to study, as if you were *tabula rasa*, an empty slate (Locke, 2001).

It is true, grounded theory has now mostly moved away from what are its arguably positivist roots towards a social constructivist understanding of societies through authors such as Strauss (in his later years), Corbin and Charmaz. However, in common with Popper (1959, 1963), I would argue that the empirical notion of inductive knowledge generating real patterns which can objectively explain society is false, and still echoes the traditions of writers such as Lazarsfeld.

Subsequently, grounded methodology was designed to lean more towards a critical rationalist approach, one that went far to acknowledge the biases of authors as they enter the field, and our "natural" tendency to generate deductive biases. These biases lead to a reliance on culturally and individually influenced forms of logic that researchers often start projects with, ones that create paradigms and then maintain them even when evidence points to the contrary. It is thus only by acknowledging these biases and working with them to compare theories with data that researchers will be able to construct a narrative that can make sense of social and cultural relationships as they are encountered.

Furthermore, grounded methodology encourages researchers to generate interpretive deduced ideas and theories that evolve through discourse during fieldwork, educational development or the design of a technology. This also makes it useful during participatory forms of practice and research if you are considering co-development of learning or co-design of technologies, for instance. In this way, by continuing the strategy of constant comparison, researchers are encouraged to develop and then investigate their own ideas as hypotheses, where data is used to constantly test and, where needed, change beliefs.

One other outcome of using the critical rationalism approach is that grounded methodology is not constrained to only "chasing" data and can be used in unique, innovative ways, which would not normally be associated with grounded studies. For example, as I show in the following paragraphs, this new flexibility and the de-emphasising of inductive logic allows grounded theory to be applied to co-creation, the development of education projects and surveys of literature.

Second, and as I pointed out earlier, a practical issue of grounded theory is that it often led to over-analysis, over-comparisons and patterns and categories so dense that they clouded and obscured coherent narratives. In addition, this cloudiness of traditional grounded theories made planning a timeframe of research difficult. Consequently, I observed that when I first tried to generate memos from my fieldnotes, they tended to produce large multi-dimensional models of patterns, categories, sub-patterns and indexes of these patterns and categories that were simply not needed.

As a result, it was decided that whilst practicing the comparison of data on relationships and categories alone, grounded methodology could more usefully form narratives that rationalised the relationships and categories that were observable in the data. This form of analysis meant that I was also observing fewer foci or a single focus of study. If enough analysis and deductive thought went into this analysis, then I could also generate a structured form of what anthropologists described as thick description, a form of analysis that had already earned its own validity (Geertz, 1989).

This change of analytical focus led to a development of the grounded methodology I was working on at the time, seeing it as the development of a story narrative for a TV drama or an everlasting play. This narrative development is outlined graphically in Figure 2.1.

In this process, the Open Coding Phase was like choosing the "characters" of your narrative, no matter whether these characters are human, institutional, policies, theories or literature. This choice of characters becomes the process of sampling considering the number of characters you need,

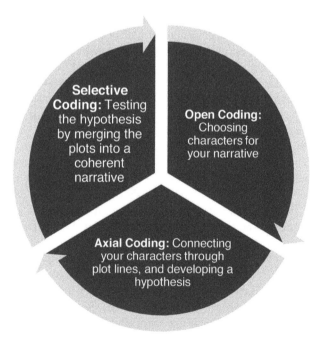

Figure 2.1 The narrative structure of a grounded methodology project

and the variables that you need to choose your characters and so forth. This sampling will be restricted to what you hope to achieve from the study and how long and wide-ranging the study is to be. The Open Coding Phase also therefore defines the life history of these characters, which can be taken forward to the Axial Coding Phase.

The Axial Coding Phase becomes analogous to the part of the narrative where the author develops what are equivalent to the plot lines of each of the characters and defines how these characters are connected. Practically, this section of the research is where the characters are clustered into categories and the relationships between and within these categories are defined and discussed critically. During this Axial Phase, this critical discussion or discourse through deductive logic and constant testing of evidence leads to the focal point of the analysis, which is the initial, tentative hypothesis.

Lastly, the Selective Coding Phase brings all of these categories and relationships from the Axial Phase and the definitions from the Open Phase together to test the hypothesis. This allows the author of the study to not only test the study but also, through new evidence, to find the greatest fallibilities of the tentative hypothesis and improve it to develop a more realistic and meaningful narrative. This narrative either stands by itself as the study, or it can move forward into a new study, where this complete narrative creates a starting point for a new deductive Open Phase of a new study.

***

What now follows are three case studies of different types of grounded methodology study, how they were constructed, their narratives and how they developed their data and evidence. All the case studies were peer-reviewed, and in two cases, these studies were funded, award-winning pieces of research.

3 Grounded methodology and field research

Simon Hayhoe, Helena Garcia Carrisoza, Jonathan Rix, Kieron Sheehy and Jane Seale

Introduction

This chapter presents a case of using grounded methodology in the field, a way of harvesting traditional grounded theory–style data and of conducting thematic analysis for a regular project. In this case, our data was harvested by testing the use of educational technologies developed for a project examining technologies and access practices for disabled people in museums. The development of this project is perhaps related to grounded theory projects you have seen previously. However, the style of analysing the data for this project is perhaps unrelated to the projects you may have read before.

The research project in this chapter was an evaluation for a project called Accessible Resources for Cultural Heritage EcoSystems (ARCHES) project, a multi-million-Euro European Union Horizon 2020–funded project that ran from 2016 to 2020. The aim of the project was to make European art and culture accessible and involved partners from six national museums (in the United Kingdom, Spain and Austria), a regional museum in Spain, four technology companies and two universities. The technology produced at the end of the project included:

an app that guides a visitor through [a] museum, accompanied by a game relating to the museum's artwork and a web platform . . . 2.5D tactile reliefs from 2D museum artefacts . . . a gesture-controlled multimedia guide including audio/text/sign language description, soundscapes, additional visual material . . . and on-screen animations . . . sign language avatars . . . apps and games on Google Play and the Apple Store, for use in the participating museums and at home. The multimedia guide [was] on display at the six participating museums (Museo Thyssen-Bornemisza in Spain, Victoria & Albert Museum in the United Kingdom, KHM-Museumsverband in Austria, Museo Lázaro Galdiano in Spain, The Wallace Collection in the United Kingdom and Museo de

Bellas Artes de Asturias in Spain) and is being marketed to European museums alongside the tactile reliefs. . . . The sign language avatar [was] developed under the EU-supported SiMAX project and . . . taken forward by the company SignTime (after the project's end date of February 2020) to improve multilingual signing-gestures.

(European Union, 2020: Paragraph 1)

Our fieldwork for the project took place in different national museums in three European capitals as well as a local museum in northern Spain: Kunsthistorisches (KHM) in Vienna, the Victoria & Albert (V&A) and Wallace Collection in London, the Museo Lázaro Galdiano and Museo Thyssen-Bornemisza in Madrid, and the Museo de Bellas Artes de Asturias in Oviedo. The three aims of this part of the research were to 1) develop recommendations in the form of Key Performance Indicators; 2) discuss the practice of design and use of technologies in cultural heritage environments; and 3) inform policies on inclusive technologies in cultural institutions (Hayhoe & Garcia Carrisoza, 2019b). All three aims were formulated with particular reference to heritage environments such as museums, monuments and national parks.

What now follows in this report is split into the following sections: 1) Context and data collection methods – this section also introduces the application of grounded methodology used in the study and the methods of collecting data; 2) The Open Coding Phase – this section analyses the results of a series of systematic literature searches, used as a foundation for the participatory research; 3) The Axial Coding Phase – this section analyses the results of interviews with participants about their experiences of ARCHES; 4) The Selective Coding Phase – this section discusses the finding of our observations and the final exercises we designed during the pilot exercises; and 5) Conclusion – this section concludes the findings we made.

Context and data collection methods

The context of ARCHES

The methodology used for ARCHES was a combination of grounded methodology and participatory research, the latter being known as participatory practice. As per the original aims of this research for ARCHES, the development of the technologies and participatory practice using technologies was based on three over-riding principles. The first principle was that access preferences were not a like-for-like replacement for impairment names or disability categories. No one on ARCHES had sensory and intellectual labels. Access preferences were what someone would choose from a long list of access options (Rix, 2007). For instance, it was previously observed that people with what was traditionally referred to as "Down syndrome" often had physical and sensory access preferences as well as learning access preferences. We also found that people with many access preferences often referred to themselves by their most important, strongest or socially most recognisable access preference, such as deafness.

In reality, it was observed that many people may have other complex needs that need to be considered as well. Thus, the negative outcome of traditional assistive technologies is that they were often designed by assuming that the user has one access need. For example, a Brailler is designed on the assumption that its user only has a visual impairment; a hearing aid is designed on the principle that the wearer may only have a hearing impairment. The outcome is the same for many accessible modern apps, which make the same basic assumption (Hayhoe, 2018). The outcome of the non-classificatory approach was an encouragement of technologies that were designed to be flexible and able to suit many access preferences. Another outcome was that technologies could often be customisable, adhering to the principle of Universal Design and adjust to changing access preferences (Thomson et al., 2015).

The second principle was the philosophical development of inclusive technologies rather than traditional forms of assistive technologies (Hayhoe, 2014a). This principle was based on the observation that traditional assistive technologies represented some of the last barriers to inclusion for disabled people, as their use was different from that of non-disabled users. For example, traditional zoom devices and cameras distinguish people with visual impairments from those without. In contrast, inclusive technology was defined in this project as:

> [A] mainstream technology that can be used with either no or minimal adaption by a person with a disability as an accessible technology. It is also seen as technology that provides social inclusion, such as communication and interaction, for [disabled people].
>
> (Hayhoe, 2014c, p. 271)

The important distinction between inclusive technologies and traditional assistive technologies was that they did not distinguish between participants. Given their inclusive nature, these technologies required the same technical skills and habits as other technology users – described in this research as technical capital (Yardi, 2009). However, the development of these specialist skills is re-defined through the use of inclusive technologies as inclusive technical capitals (Hayhoe, 2019a).

Given these guiding principles and the trends in technology usage and their size and lightness, mobile technologies such as smartphones and tablet computers were identified as the best devices for this project. This was not possible in all situations, however, as it was not feasible to make many tactile technologies mobile at the time. Therefore, technological development during the project created new augmented technologies to translate to the needs of inclusive technologies, with many paradoxes still existing.

The third principle of this project was the use of augmented and cross-modal forms of learning wherever possible. In particular, ARCHES used the principle that augmented reality used multiple forms of media to develop alternative environments and ways of perceiving and learning about the outside world (Sheehy et al., 2014). These different and alternative views were most commonly delivered at the time through approximations to Virtual Reality (VR) technologies.

Similarly, cross-modal cognition was seen as the way that cultural heritage visitors interpret and integrate sensory information to develop a single *image* of the outside world (Spence, 2010), or through a cross-modal understanding of the outside world in combination with language (Hayhoe et al., 2019).

This latter form of technology was particularly important for those research participants with perceptual and learning disabilities, as substituting or enhancing touch, sound or sight for those with such preferences could enhance learning. In practice, ARCHES worked on the principle that this idea of developing augmented reality by tailoring sensory input for those with a variety of access preferences enhanced the capacity to understand museum environments and exhibits (Neumüller & Reichinger, 2013).

Data collection methods

In this project we had to learn to be reflexive. Unfortunately, much of the technology was not finished in time to present three distinct phases of research. Some technologies, such as a sign-language avatar, were not developed enough by mid-2019 to test, and another piece of software which was supposed to be developed called Our Story was not available at all. Therefore, the strategy of the researchers was adapted to reflect this lack of testing.

The subsequent research therefore examined the broader picture of technological development and multi-sensory activities in situ. This included examining the use of our most-used technologies, such as the tablet computers, projectors and mobile telephones, the hands-on activities undertaken within the groups and the academic literature in this field. Eventually, after adapting our research study, the data collection methods were ordered into logical strands of data development and analysis that we could use in a three-phased thematic analysis. These three phases of research were:

1 Systematic literature reviews of academic literature on participation, design, e-learning, the use of augmented reality in museums and m-learning in museums. This exercise also identified a possible analytical framework that could focus the analysis in phases two and three.
2 Interviews with participants (these were translated by expert professional translators in Austria and Spain), observations of partner and mainstream inclusive technologies and tools used during participant sessions and the results of pilot tests and consultations with participants. At the end of this section, an initial hypothesis was formulated and taken forward to be tested in the third phase, as with all grounded methodologies.
3 A formal consultation exercise with participants in museums in London and Vienna. The first part of this exercise asked the participants what they thought about the different parts of the analytical framework developed earlier, which was broken down into approachable language. The second part of the exercise was to ask the participants to design or describe what their ultimate technology would be, based on their experiences in the groups. It should also be noted that the exercises in Vienna were interpreted by a professional translator as the participant running the exercises was a native English speaker.

The following is a discussion of the results of this data analysis.

The Open Coding Phase

Four literature searches focusing on the design and use of technologies for people with access preferences in cultural institutions were developed during the early stages of this phase. These reviews included:

1 A review of literature on Augmented Reality (AR) in cultural heritage environments (Sheehy et al., 2019).
2 Two reviews of literature on the design of technologies for people with learning disabilities and sensory impairments in cultural heritage environments (Rix et al., 2019; Seale et al., 2018).
3 A review on the practice and development of mobile technologies in the process of learning through the use of technologies in cultural heritage environments (Hayhoe et al., 2019).

As these are published elsewhere, the data from these individual studies will only be summarised as follows.

Review of the Literature on Augmented Reality (AR): In this review, we found that AR technologies were discussed in multiple formats in the literature, but that a single paradigm or over-riding model of use was yet to evolve. Importantly, we found AR was mainly used for mobile data connections, for multi-sensory media, text-to-speech applications and, less commonly, for haptic telepresence (that is, having a touch representation of an object in a different location). Some literature also suggested that museum visitors were able to share AR experiences in real time via social networks through their own choice of personal technology and social media.

In addition, we observed that the majority of inclusive AR technologies discussed in the literature were designed to support visitors with visual impairments, although other access preferences were supported to a lesser extent through separate technologies. For instance, there is mention of devices that aided navigation within the museums and supported people with learning disabilities to get to the site itself or technologies that provided support through robotics. This seemed to suggest that many AR devices still supported traditional models of assistive technologies and designed technologies for individual access preferences.

Moreover, we also found that there was a lack of focus on the needs of Deaf, deaf and hearing-impaired people in the literature. We felt that this was because text technologies were becoming commercially available, live translation systems were well established and signing avatars were found in apps. So, few technologies were developed as *standalone technologies*. Problems with usefully deploying and integrating these technologies into museum experiences are also found in the literature.

During an analysis of the uneven development of AR, we identified eight important *affordances* or relationships to the use of AR that could be measured against a scale of ability. These affordances were: Collaboration, Connectivity, Authenticity, Multi-Sensory Media, Student-Centred Technologies, Shared Knowledge, Community and Exploration. In the literature survey, it was also observed that Connectivity and Authenticity impaired the development of augmented learning more than other affordances did. For instance, Community and Student-Centred Technologies and Shared Knowledge were found to be most important to the design of successful technologies.

Reviews of Literature on the Design Process for Learning and Sensory Access Preferences: In these reviews we found that the literature tended to use generic, standardised design techniques, principles of Universal Design (that is, designs and tools that suited a majority of user needs), minimised specialist tools and their designers did not explicitly address a need to ensure accessibility. Unfortunately, we also found that the absence of detailed justifications in this literature also made it difficult to draw firm conclusions that could demonstrate an epistemological trend and a paradigm of design that could be evaluated. Subsequently, we observed that many technologies favoured generic designs and users with sensory impairments over users with learning disabilities. In addition, we also observed that where these issues were considered, designers preferred specialist designs for users with learning disabilities.

These reviews also observed that generic design techniques tended to be employed by disabled designers and stakeholders, who also involved disabled people in their design process. Thus, we found that using significant amounts of participation and hybridised approaches to working with users with access preferences led to more engagement and a commitment to inclusion. Much of the literature mentioning the experience of working with participatory design also found that designers working with users with access preferences learnt about the needs of their users, users with access preferences as a whole and themselves. However, as with the review of literature on AR, we could not identify a clear overall picture of paradigms or models of design and development in these reviews, perhaps because this was a young topic of investigation at the time.

After these two reviews, we met as a team and felt that more evidence to support the initial analysis and the tentative conclusions made by this literature was needed. Furthermore, this field needed to consider developing robust paradigms that could further develop research and allow future literature reviews to examine clear frameworks via a range of access preferences. Areas we thought could benefit from this form of evaluation were the design of technologies favouring participatory design practices with users with sensory impairments and the explicit and detailed decision-making processes that technology designers made.

In order to try to formalise these future directions of research, a model of analysis was developed that could be used as a starting process to evaluate design practices and literature. This model was composed of the four broad elements listed as follows, and developed into Table 3.1, which shows suggested user groups these elements could be applied to:

Designing for usability in a defined environment and for a defined practice – Is about ensuring people with access preferences can easily use the technology and this use is unimpeded.

Designing for accessibility to the audience for which it is intended – Is about ensuring people with access preferences can easily access the content or experience being offered by the technology, thus reducing barriers to meaningful engagement with the content or experience.

Table 3.1 A comprehensive framework for the design of technologies for people with learning difficulties

Diversity & Difference/Digital Inclusion	USE	ACCESS	EMPOWERMENT	PARTICIPATION
Designing for anyone – disabled or non-disabled	Usability design principles			
Designing for anyone who is disabled	Usability design principles	Accessibility design principles		
Designing for anyone who is disempowered or excluded	Usability design principles	Accessibility design principles	Agency design principles	
Designing for anyone with a learning difficulty	Usability design principles	Accessibility design principles	Agency design principles	Learning Support design principles

Designing for agency, to empower its intended users through its practice – Is about ensuring people with access preferences can exert some control over the content or the experience being offered by the technology.

Designing for Learning Support, which is to develop participation in the development of the technology – Is about ensuring people with access preferences can learn something from the content or the experience being offered by the technology and, in doing so, participate in an active way in the arts, rather than being passive consumers of heritage and cultural sites.

Review of the Literature on Learning Practices Using Technologies: In common with the aforementioned reviews, we observed that teaching and learning strategy for disabled learners in cultural heritage environments was a greatly under-researched field. In addition, the literature as a whole had failed to develop its own research models that could be tested by robust evaluations at the point the survey was conducted. This said, we found that the existing literature supported the inclusion agenda of cultural institutions through the use of three applications of technology: 1) the pedagogical use of fixed technologies, which allowed for cross-modal interaction with exhibits; 2) the redesign of exhibits to make them more interactive and academically stimulating through augmented technologies; and 3) the development of discourses on museum exhibits using social networks.

However, we also found that early evaluations identified three significant weaknesses in the current teaching and learning strategies and their use of technologies. Firstly, we found that the design of teaching and learning lacks agency for those involved in the education or design or use of the technology. In particular, there was a lack of involvement of people with access preferences in the development of their own education. Secondly, we felt that there was little coherence in the management of inclusive learning, and there seemed to be a lack of standardisation or a holistic understanding of the use of technologies in the education of people with access preferences. Thirdly, we found that although the literature had moved forward in its understanding of access, teaching and learning using technologies still focused on individual impairments and favoured a deficit model of users with access preferences.

***

As a team of researchers, we learnt two lessons from all four literature reviews, which we took forward to the second phase of research. The first and most significant lesson was that there is no overall understanding of design for all engineers, educators and app developers of the needs of people with access preferences. Secondly, there was also a significant difference between disparate professions, such as educators, designers and engineers, although they also share a significant need to develop technologies that provided agency for people with access preferences. These findings and the framework were taken forward to the analysis in the Axial Coding Phase – in this chapter, we are concentrating on certain parts of this framework as this whole analysis was large.

The Axial Coding Phase

Agency difficult to find

In general, we found that agency was difficult to observe during testing and observations of the use of technologies in situ. However, during ARCHES, the most observable element of agency was the recognition of feedback from participants leading to changes. For instance, agency was observable when discussing the contents of artworks during sessions that examined the ability of artworks to *tell a story*. In these circumstances, we found that the participants particularly appreciated being involved in the process of choosing artworks and the language that was used to describe each piece in the apps, as it made the importance of their voices apparent. Furthermore, there were other examples of mobile technologies that could develop agency and knowledge amongst the participants during the broader work in the sessions.

In addition, during our observations we found that the participants in the museums liked to use technologies to record their own participation in the group, to make notes and to develop their own understanding of processes. In some instances, participants had been encouraged to record their experiences and observations prior to attending the groups. Importantly, we felt that this allowed the participants an opportunity to develop their own *participatory voice*. For example, during one session we observed that:

> [A Participant] takes the iPad from the table in its case, and starts going around the table unobtrusively taking pictures of the group. She puts the iPad back away from the table on a table to the side.

However, we also observed that two issues needed further research to improve Agency: 1) cultural appropriateness of the representation of the access preferences, disability and the ethnicity of participants; and 2) the use of language that prevented full engagement with participation. This led us to develop two sub-strands of observation during the sessions in the museums.

Cultural Appropriateness and Representation: One of the main issues mentioned during discussions on the use of avatars and other forms of animated character was the cultural stereotyping of the characters. This issue seemed particularly acute in London, where participants were representative of numerous ethnicities. For instance, as one participant observed of characters in the storyboard of an animation:

> [Everyone] is a lovely shade of "white." I appreciate the story-board is short but surely some diversity could be included.
>
> Likewise, in respect to the representation of disabled people I assume that the blond man in the dark glasses . . . is supposed to represent a blind person? I appreciate that it would be impossible to represent every disability or impairment within the story-board, so why not represent us with the universal symbol.

Related concerns were mooted in Madrid during a discussion on numerous symbols used to represent disabled people on instruction sheets. As was noted during one observation, "Some of the symbols on the sheet are criticised for being offensive, particularly to 'blind and deaf people.'"

The Use of Language and Images Preventing Participation in Design: Conversely, we also observed that *inappropriate* forms of language or the use of images led to feelings of exclusion from participatory conversations on the design of technologies by participants. For example, in the London participatory sessions, participants made comments that some of the texts for the technologies initially made them feel excluded, as it was too complex. In addition, during discussions on the exhibits, we observed that the use of text in conjunction with images made it difficult for some participants to contribute to the design of the technology. This was recorded in observational notes as follows:

> [There are comments about the text] on screen being too long and not "easy read" and the typeface being too small. At one point, [a participant] also has to go to [another participant with a visual impairment to describe texts] that have not been described to him as the talk is given to provide a verbal description. . . . [Presenter] is talking, [participant with visual impairments] sits still and quiet. [Presenter] has a great number of images, and she gestures over them to show the features. [Participant with visual impairments] remains quiet and does not engage with the group.

Difficulties in analysing learning support

As with Agency, it was difficult to gauge the extent to which technologies developed Learning Support in the form of new knowledge and skills, as no instruments of measuring learning were used during ARCHES. However, it became apparent that the casual use of technologies taught participants to search for information that enabled and developed further self-directed skills and knowledge and formed personal inclusion; these skills and knowledge were termed *inclusive capitals* (Hayhoe, 2019b) during an earlier topical review for ARCHES – the model of inclusive capital is discussed in greater detail in the next chapter.

For instance, during numerous participant sessions, we found that search functions were used casually to search for information and to discuss different elements of access and inclusion. In this way, there appeared to be a relationship between Learning Support and Agency within participatory settings, with inclusive capitals being largely premised on finding mainstream information. The following excerpt, for example, illustrates a session from Madrid where a number of participants were asked to comment on images that were used for a project app.

> During our conversation we use the iPad as a reference point for finding [images to be used in technologies]. We use a regular Google search

engine to identify the correct image, which has to be very precise. [We find a sign for deafness, which has been discussed previously.] . . . The tablet computer is passed between the participants, which allows for quick comparisons. It also causes a talking point . . . and allows us to compare information quickly.

One significant design element that facilitated Learning Support was the ability of technologies to transform information for participants. In particular, many participants felt it was important to integrate alternative forms of communication according to menu preferences that could subsequently provide different ways and a greater depth of learning. This issue was found to reduce stress for some participants. For example, in a message to TreeLogic early in the development of ARCHES, and acting on feedback from participants, different interfaces including different forms of knowledge and information were felt to be necessary for some participants:

[Question] for TreeLogic:

> Would it be possible to develop two interfaces attending to participant's preferences: one simpler (with all the information in the same page and the link of more info at the end) and a different one that includes different sections/icons next to short description where you can click into to know more?

During participatory exercises, we found there was also evidence that technologies helped to develop empathy and an understanding of others' access preferences during the course of using the partner technologies. However, despite this increased knowledge there still appeared to be a bar between the use of these technologies and the opinions of participants that certain forms of access settings were "for someone else." Consequently, we found that the traditional culture of separate assistive technologies for single impairments, what can be referred to as *a culture of separation*, may form a cultural block that may take time to overcome. For example, in an interview with a participant from London, it appeared that they found it difficult to use technologies for participants solely with visual impairments, although this difficulty made them reflect on their own understanding of visual impairment.

> I don't like using the eye things because it was horrible, but it made me think of the fact of if you're blind that's what your vision would be and so just to touch the object for that few minutes I would use them, but not for the whole time and that was good for me because I haven't really understood my cousin, who is blind.

Initial hypothesis

Building on these findings, we formulated a hypothesis that could be taken forward to the Selective Phase to triangulate the early findings. This hypothesis was as follows:

> The technologies that were tested or used during ARCHES were largely successful in developing elements of the four stages of the Analytical Framework produced in phase one of the analysis – i.e. they were largely Usable, Accessible, and developed Agency and Learning Support. However, other more specialist issues arose that related to technologies and a range of access preferences. In particular, some access preferences were not based on the physical, sensory or cognitive needs of the participants, but on social or cultural needs. In addition, there were other practical issues and issues of well-being that needed further consideration that needed to be added to the Analytical Framework.

The Selective Coding Phase

As we stated earlier, the exercise that resulted in the findings of the Selective Phase was in two parts:

> **Part 1:** Participants from groups in London and Vienna were asked what they thought of the Analytical Framework identified in phase one of the research, with the exercise in Vienna being supported by an English- and German-speaking translator. Their comments were based on their personal experiences of testing the technologies that were developed during ARCHES and their use of the other technologies used in museums.
>
> **Part 2:** The groups were also asked to design or describe an ultimate technology that could be used by their host museum. Similarly, this technology and its features were meant to be based on their experience of using and evaluating technologies over the course of ARCHES and their personal experiences in museums. Many of the participants decided to describe rather than draw designs, although many chose to draw their designs.

We felt that the results of this exercise largely supported the hypothesis. Furthermore, the model Analytical Framework was partly seen as a good framework for developing Key Performance Indicators, as participants felt the issues in the framework were partly important; although there was some difference in what they thought of as more or less important, with

Accessibility the most important and Agency and Learning Support being of lesser importance.

However, as the second phase of analysis did, there were further observations that had not appeared in the literature and subsequently had not been integrated into the Analytical Framework. Furthermore, different relationships between the elements of the Analytical Framework were expressed by the participants that differed largely from the Analytical Framework. Subsequently, our analysis came to focus on relationships between different elements of the framework and issues that were not included in the original framework.

Accessibility a significant issue

We found that accessibility was the most discussed topic during the exercises, with the issue of an emotional relationship to technologies arising a number of times; and within this broader issue, two sub-issues were again identified by participants. The first sub-issue participants identified was the ability to choose the amount and type of information, and the emotional relationship they had *with the information* through their interface. For instance, one participant mentioned that when they listened to audio descriptions, they liked to make their own decisions about how much text they would like, what the information they received was and the type of "ambient noise" they preferred. Other participants, particularly those with hearing impairments, felt that the type of voices used in voice-to-text also needed *more personality*. For instance, their understanding of the sounds they preferred was not simply based on levels of hearing, but also on the empathy voices engendered and how comfortable they made them feel. In one instance, a participant mentioned the need for a person with a soft voice and simple wording in a text-to-speech function, as this was less threatening to her as a user.

However, as with all the other issues discussed, some participants preferred an opposite, "tougher approach" that could help develop resilience. In particular, for some participants, the harder they tried to become accustomed to unfamiliar technologies, the greater resilience they built and the greater sense of achievement they felt. Subsequently, it was observable that there was a strong relationship between the tougher approach to accessibility and the learning support elements of the analytical framework that were discussed afterwards. As one participant recalled:

[When] we started the multi-media project, how hard was it for people? Because, it was really hard . . . but when we started to do the project, we had so much fun with it, didn't we? We had pictures, we had something to write. And so, we could send something to [Other Participant]. That was the whole exercise.

The second sub-issue raised by the participants in Vienna and London was the simplicity and familiarity of the technologies' interfaces. In particular, participants often said that they needed inclusive technologies to bear a relationship to old-fashioned technologies they had used. For example, in descriptions of interfaces for the ultimate technology, participants mentioned having buttons instead of touchscreen technologies. Again, this was unrelated to their access preference; it just seemed more familiar to them. Furthermore, several participants also preferred to have familiar sounds such as those you would hear on contemporary technologies or media devices, such as a familiar person or the sound of typing or the sound of a photographic click. As one participant commented:

> I would rather hear someone. But, I would do it a different way, and I think other people would as well.

In addition, and again we found that this was unrelated to their regular access preferences, some participants described an inclination to tactile elements of interfaces that were physically and emotionally comforting. As one participant told us, "[It needs to feel] reassuring, comforting, soothing." In a further example, one participant's design integrated several colorful, tactile and multi-media elements that could be used as a welcoming device in the entrance of the museum:

> This could go at the front entrance of the museum, so that's what this picture is about. . . . So, for example, it should have three pages: a book, a picture and a green button. The green button people can actually press and words will come up. . . . If someone could feel it, it would be furry, so people could feel it and see the text. . . . And there could be patterns, and less writing – it should be in easy read.

Agency and Learning Support correlated

We found that Agency and Learning Support were the least recognisable issues related to inclusive technologies by the participants during the exercise. Where agency was mentioned, it was often related to issues of hearing impairment, and where learning support was mentioned, it was often related to issues of the amount and type of information available. Although, as in the second phase of analysis, issues of Agency and Learning Support were sometimes correlated. For instance, a number of participants felt that having sign language empowered Deaf signers, who sometimes preferred to see themselves as a distinct language community. Other participants felt that technology which provided too much emphasis on signing or de-emphasised the needs of non-signers who nevertheless had hearing impairments removed agency. For instance, during the exercises, one participant told us that signing was often seen as the only need people with hearing impairments were thought to have in technologies used by museums:

> The main point is, I don't think that any aspect of deafness is still being looked into. I mean, yes, it's OK to have [the signer] but if you come here [to a museum] on your own, you would need help to know where to go to look at a certain thing.

On learning support, we also found that participants had differing opinions on how much information should be made available. Some participants liked all the information to be shown, with them then being able to sift teaching materials available in apps themselves and decide what they wanted. On the other hand, a number of participants preferred introducing information and teaching materials slowly or bit by bit. As one participant told us:

> A little bit is good, but too much is too much. It's sometimes too much for you to develop and formulate your own thoughts . . . they want to see the art, they want to have a bit of information, but they want it to be short and concise.

Similarly, there were different access preferences about the practice of learning in the museum, with participants correlating the style of learning support with elements of Agency. For instance, some participants preferred to be provided with concepts and ideas about artworks, where their ideas could be taken further and they could decide how to use the information themselves. We found that this provided participants with a sense of empowerment and allowed them a say in their own learning objectives. As one participant stated:

> Discovering new things is important, and facilitating things you have done before is important.

However, we also found that other participants preferred to "have fun in the museum," and did not want to worry about having to deal with too much information, finding there was value in having choices. Some participants also told us they would like information before they get to museums, so they could decide what they would like when they got there.

> You go to a museum in your free time, when you want to have fun, for example. And, it's nice to have *some* information.

Support and advocacy, well-being and awareness of technologies emerged

The first of the additional issues that were discussed by participants was the need to consider third parties acting as supporters or advocates. Thus, in this instance, Advocacy was thought of as the ability to communicate for others, to make sure their rights were considered or what they say is heard. For example, one participant identified an app she had on her smartphone that allowed multiple conversations for signers or for those who found verbal communication difficult. The signer featured on the app was a human interface that could both communicate and advocate for the user if needed:

> I'm OK, but there are people who can't speak. There's an app here, and it's basically an interpreter and you can get a three-way conversation. There will be an interpreter who takes what is typed in to say what a person wants. So, there are lots of bits and pieces to allow people to get what they need.[1]

The other issue that participants mooted during the exercise was the stress and threat to well-being that some of their technologies could cause. For example, one participant explained how she found the ownership of technologies threatening for a long time, an issue that was exasperated by media coverage of threats to personal security, personal finances and finding inappropriate material. It was only when she had an incident that could potentially cause extreme stress that she decided to get a smartphone, and from then on, a computer. From this point on, she found that a supporter's ongoing help improved her opinion of mainstream technologies, building her confidence in the use of technology as she did so.

> Because for a very, very long time I refused to have a computer. . . . But, I had someone come in with me once a week, helping me with stuff. And, it's been really, really good.
>   But, it was very difficult for me in the first place. I was worried about getting lots of things that I didn't want to get into. You know, about all that stuff you get on the dark Web, and stuff like that. And, I didn't want to do anything like that, that's why I refused to have a computer.

Another participant told us about a related fear of technology but found that attending ARCHES to learn about museum technologies had increased her confidence in their use. In addition, she found that using technologies and developing soft skills also gave her the confidence to develop further skills, such as electronic communication, and subsequently take on solo projects and exercises during the project.

I used to have a fear of technology. Not understanding how to use emails. And, not understanding how to use anything. But, I've taught myself. And I still do get it [a fear of technology], but I don't get it as much as I used to.

It is this project that's got me out of my fear. Because I had a fear of the iPad and looking in the museums and not knowing how to use an iPad. I [have overcome a] fear of going around the museum with it [an iPad], and writing notes on it and things, and looking up a presentation on it.

The third issue raised was one of awareness of technology. This issue was first mooted in the design of the ultimate technologies, where it was felt that technologies should be advertised to potential users. Other participants described how they wanted the technologies they designed to be put on front desks or by entrances to museums, so these technologies would be the first thing visitors saw when they entered the building. However, the most telling description of raising a general awareness of inclusive technologies in museums, we felt, came out of discussions that occurred in groups with the participants. As one participant explained during one of these group discussions:

The first thing I would like to know is what is the availability of the apps when I first enter the museum. Who tells me we have an app. The availability and who or what tells me that this app is available for this museum is the first issue I conjure.

Conclusion

Despite their best intentions, many traditional assistive technologies often reinforced the exclusion of disabled people. Furthermore, largely because of stereotypical ideas about disability, these technologies often only focused on single impairments and fell short of providing wide-ranging inclusion. Historically, these separate technologies caused numerous problems, not least of which was a culture of technical separation that meant many disabled people either shunned these separate technologies or were caught up in a separate culture of only being able to use these devices. Subsequently, many users only developed skills related to assistive technologies and not mainstream technologies, and found it difficult to adapt to their technologies in a mainstream environment.

Contemporary technologies, with accessible and inclusive settings built into their operating systems, particularly mobile wireless technologies such as smartphones and tablets, have disrupted this exclusion. Moreover, they have changed the philosophy of such technologies, from one of a notion of assistance of those considered to be incapable of using mainstream technologies to one of technological inclusion. Subsequently, over the past decade, new and inclusive mainstream devices have become almost ubiquitous for those who previously shunned technologies.

And yet, largely because of the youth of these new technologies, academic literature has failed to change its culture meaningfully and develop frameworks or instruments by which inclusive technologies can be measured. ARCHES attempted to change this culture. However, this project also identified further issues that do not appear in previous literature and also found that the importance of the factors making up the analytical framework differ, with usability and accessibility being seen as disproportionately more important to participants in this study than agency and learning support. Therefore, our understanding of inclusive technology has had to evolve in order to reflect this feedback.

So, what is the next stage in this process?

Importantly, further research needs to be conducted into the issue of inclusive technologies for use in cultural institutions. Although ARCHES has started this process, it is unable to account for all contexts and all access needs, and therefore its findings need further development. In addition, cultural institutions need to develop further strategies and policies that lead to cultural and political change in their institutions. This is most important, as without this political will, the development of inclusive technologies will not evolve, users will not develop confidence in their use and participation will not lead to fundamental changes.

Acknowledgement

This project has received funding from the European Union's Horizon 2020 research and innovation programme under grant agreement No 693229 – Appendix A.

Note

1 It should also be noted that early in the London group, researchers tried to find technologies that would convert text into sign language and speech into text. This function was requested in technologies such as Our Story, but this never appeared.

4 Grounded methodology and developing education

Introduction

In this chapter, I focus on the design, development and evaluation of a public education project that attempted to develop relationships between communities in the city of Bath and local artists to create a grounded methodology. The project was called River is the Venue (RiV) and used grounded methodology to commission artists and recruit community participants to develop public, sensorially and intellectually accessible artworks. These artworks were designed to educate people throughout the city of Bath about local flood events. RiV's participant stakeholders included disabled people, members of the local community, civil engineers, scientists, arts educators, a local arts centre and a local arts charity based in the city's hospital.

Although I had previously used grounded methodology to develop experimental adult education courses and undergraduate training sessions prior to RiV (see, for example, Hayhoe et al., 2017; Hayhoe et al., 2015), this new project was unique. It combined grounded methodology as a structure to develop participatory practice, which resulted in the co-creation of its artworks and learning strategies. The specific topics of these artworks and learning strategies was the *social and cultural history of flooding*, ranging from the eighteenth century through to the early millennium, and the *use of engineering to control flooding*.

Overall, RiV had two main aims: 1) to explore the development of sensorially and intellectually accessible public artworks through the experiences of artists-as-co-teachers, and how this experience informs these artists' present and future practice; and 2) to examine the commissioning of public artworks as a means of socially inclusive public education, as the commissions for RiV were designed to make the medium of public artworks physically, socially and academically closer to their audiences

RiV also examined the encouragement of artists and their use of multimodal pedagogies as tools of teaching communities through different senses to re-create the visual, aural and tactile image of the river, along with an experience of its tastes and smells. Thus, the knowledge that the artists communicated was also designed to be interactive through performance and audience participation, and related to art projects developed prior to and simultaneously with this project (see for example, Hayhoe, 2013a; Hayhoe & Garcia Carrisoza, 2019b).

This chapter has five sections following this introduction: 1) Context and the three stages of RiV – this section discusses the theoretical motivation for the project and discusses the method of designing, developing and evaluating RiV; 2) The Open Coding Phase – this section discusses the development of participatory groups, the examination of theory and the original development of a framework or model of analysis; 3) The Axial Coding Phase – this section develops the framework or model of analysis, its application in the development of the project and the hypothesis that resulted from this work; 4) The Selective Coding Phase – this section presents the evaluation of RiV, measured against the hypothesis that was formulated during the Axial Coding Phase; and 5) Conclusion – this section concludes the experiences and analysis of RiV.

Context and the three stages of RiV

The context of RiV

Traditionally, public artworks were often commissioned to inspire national cultures, political or religious ideology or power, and were related to a permanent geographical space that reflected this status (Mitchell, 1990; Johnson, 1995; Levinson, 2018). Subsequently, rather than making the public feel closer to these figures, these artworks were often placed up high, out of reach of their viewers, or they were designed to make the public feel a sense of reverence rather than a *sense of inclusion*. Furthermore, as they were placed physically away from their audience, traditional public artworks were often inaccessible to those with disabilities such as visual impairment and restricted mobility (Argyropoulos & Kanari, 2015).

During the latter years of the twentieth century, the subjects of public artworks changed to move closer to the public imagination. These subjects included less elevated issues and ideas, communicated a broader range of beliefs and represented a broader spectrum of humanity and religious ideals (Hall & Robertson, 2001). Subsequently, the philosophy of commissioning artworks also changed to engender less reverence, to develop more social debate and communicate untraditional feelings or messages. Yet, despite these changes, public artworks still often inadvertently excluded viewers, mainly because these viewers were physically, intellectually or socially less able to access these artworks (Smith et al., 2013).

During RiV, we aimed to examine public artworks in different ways and to include the community in different stages of project development. More importantly, during RiV we specifically intended to commission artworks that were largely, consciously accessible to disabled people and other marginalised members of the community. In doing so, its objective was to encourage commissioned artists to examine a *sense of inclusion* amongst more marginalised communities, and for these communities to develop an alternative understanding of the dangers of flooding.

Subsequently, the project's outputs were eventually to evolve and include an interactive digital platform; a guided trail with artworks relating to historic flooding events along the River Avon, the river that runs through the centre of Bath; hydraulic models of selected cross-sections of the River Avon representing historic flood events; reconstructed evidence of the social history of the River Avon; and accessible and inclusive exhibitions and the project's story created by various members of the community that lived and studied near the river. These outcomes were to largely relate to community engagement, through the creation of physically and culturally accessible art spaces for the local community, and to encourage discussion about its themes.

Eventually, we also purposely designed and developed this project with several outcomes in mind, which were: 1) to reach out to non-conventional audiences who had not participated during its development and who would not normally engage with public artworks; 2) to show the potential quality of art as an educational tool for Science Technology Engineering and Mathematics (STEM) related topics; and 3) to begin a broader debate on flood management strategies and establish collaborations across a unique range of local stakeholders.

During the project, the stakeholders, who were our participants, were to include art spaces, schools, colleges, local universities, care home residents, patient groups, the city council, local disability organisations, community groups and local water companies. During RiV, we decided to combine the expertise and experiences of these local, disabled expert participants to curate and exhibit artworks, and to guide and create its multi-sensory artworks. In addition, participants who took part early on also guided the nature of the commissions we made.

We found that this approach to participation also provided a foundation for interdisciplinary research between academics, such as civil engineers and arts educators. Furthermore, we found that this approach also formed a basis for research that went beyond single academic disciplines. Thus, RiV included elements of education, civil engineering, fine art and musical theory. This approach was also intended to inform all phases of the project, from the formulation of the artworks through to the evaluation of the

processes involved in developing the artworks and how it changed participants' opinions of learning.

The interactive character of RiV also encouraged teamwork, contribu-
tions and the involvement of different participants at multiple stages of
the project, not just in the creation of artworks or their initial ideas. For
instance, the artists became part of a panel to discuss the artworks with
members of the public during research nights. To encourage this practice,
RiV purposely commissioned a range of artworks based on numerous
medias, styles and genres. These genres included contemporary sculptural
pieces to avant-garde musical composition and performance, performative
puppet theatre and a series of art education workshops. The workshops in
particular encouraged the artists to interact with members of the local community to participate in creating their own public artworks and engender a
sense of ownership in the project.

The three phases of design, development and evaluation

The methodology used to develop and evaluate RiV was again unusual, as
it mixed grounded methodology with participatory practice, a combination
I used in ARCHES (Hayhoe & Garcia Carrisoza, 2019a). In this study, the
Open Phase consisted of designing a theoretical model of knowledge-transfer
and evaluation for the project. That is, this phase was building a theoretical instrument through which participants could implement and measure
learning, knowledge-transfer and development. In addition, in this phase we
conducted participatory meetings with stakeholders during Winter 2017–
2018. However, this was the first time this methodology was applied to
professional public artworks as an instrument of teaching. The theoretical
model was also conducted in conjunction with a model of study which was
developed for ARCHES.

The Axial Phase took the evolution of this theoretical model further,
whilst working within the boundaries of the aim of the project to support
the learning of unrepresented learners. The Axial Phase thus transformed
the theoretical model into an accessible and inclusive learning strategy
for knowledge-transfer, based on the evidence gathered during participant
meetings during the Open Phase. This approach eventually led to a more
focused learning strategy during Spring 2018, when we finally implemented
our axial coding workplan. This strategy included:

- a call for artists, focusing on a need for inclusion and public access
- the commissioning of an accessible website to promote the artworks
  and contribute to the learning and knowledge-transfer of the project
- the development of artworks based on modes of accessibility
- the exhibition of the mechanical pieces related to flooding research

The knowledge-transfer in particular was in part based on recent experiences of participatory research groups and related different experiences of accessing artworks in museums (Hayhoe & Garcia Carrisoza, 2019a). From this theoretical perspective, we eventually developed our hypothesis to conduct the evaluation, which again considered the original aims of the project.

To implement the evaluation of the project during the Selective Phase and to test our hypothesis, we used three data collection methods: 1) photographs of making the projects and exhibits in situ; 2) interviews with the participating artists; and 3) a review of questionnaires for those participating in initial participatory sessions, which were reviewed in retrospect. The questionnaire was created and returned in MS Word and used open questions which invited protracted answers. We chose MS Word as it is largely accessible to people with disabilities, and it is used and understood by a large proportion of the population. The questions forming the surveys were split into two, with the first set asking participants about their professional histories and the second half asking about their experiences of participating in the project.

The methodology was conducted in accordance with the British Educational Research Association's guidelines on ethical research (BERA, 2018) and evaluated by the Faculty of Humanities and Social Science, University of Bath, for its ethical appropriateness. Thus, participation in the participatory sessions and the commissioning of artworks by the stakeholders and artists was wholly voluntary. The participants were also invited to participate through previously established contacts in order to comply with these ethical procedures. Furthermore, during the study, participants were given consent forms before they filled out interviews and questionnaires. During and after the interviews, participants were also offered the opportunity to withdraw, although over the course of the participatory consultations, no participants asked to withdraw. During the project, apart from the payment to the artists for their commissions and materials, we also consciously placed no coercion on the participants through incentives or payments.

The Open Coding Phase

Models of learning through developing human value

As stated earlier, this study was conducted in parallel with the ARCHES project I discussed in the last chapter. As a part of ARCHES, I was developing and discussing a model of social and cultural inclusion with a number of academics in partner projects as a development of a previous model designed for technology (Hayhoe et al., 2015), and this new model was first presented at a conference to gauge feedback (Hayhoe et al., 2017).

This fed into a re-review of literature in this field, part of which I had conducted for previous projects. During this re-review of previous theories and the ideas they were based on, I observed that philosophies of human value have evolved chronologically since the Enlightenment (Hayhoe, 2019b). Furthermore, human value, referred to as intangible skills and habits by Bourdieu (2010) and Yardi (2009, 2010), was felt to be an effective way of understanding our personal knowledge, activities and skills.

The variables in this literature were also thought to influence how these elements shape our personality, memory and characters. Likewise, writers since the eighteenth century had theorised that human values shape individual identity, behaviour, motives and desires and shape informal knowledge (Hayhoe, 2019b). In addition, I concluded that these previous philosophies of human values have a single common theme: they value a *sense of inclusion* for a category of people as part of our human condition to feel part of a network. That is, they hypothesise the value of family, friends, social class, religion and ethnicity as a community.

Subsequently, these philosophies appeared to show us that networking and learning were instinctive, something that my colleagues and I observed in our own research projects and professional practice. That is, although there are better and worse ways of networking and learning, and we might be encouraged to use one way over another, because we are not specifically taught to network and learn, we simply network and learn on our own. Networking and learning are therefore arguably part of our human condition of developing a *sense of inclusion*.

Models of capital as knowledge and habits

Yardi's (2009) model of technical capital, which itself evolved out of a model of cultural capital, demonstrated it is not only important to get information and use it to feel included. Information is part of our human history to develop and use technologies and the arts, just as it can also be said to be part of our history to seek out our heritage and the heritage of others. Thus, cultural capital, which was first described by Bourdieu (2010), can also be knowing when to use certain types of language, such as internet jargon, and with whom certain language is socially acceptable.

More controversially, human capital can be seen as our moral and immoral knowledge, such as our rules about how to exclude others who don't fit our own rules of social acceptability. It could also be said that it is part of our human character to seek out inclusion as a value, to feel our *sense of inclusion*, and thus this inclusion fosters our sense of value (Hayhoe, 2019b). Consequently, to develop inclusive capital can also be central to our human history, as it provides us with a *sense of value*. Thus, this *sense of value* and *sense of inclusion* became the atomic level of the model of inclusive capital.

During this project, it was felt that acquiring inclusive capital was especially important for disabled people, older people and people feeling a sense of marginalisation. For example, people with disabilities are more likely to find barriers to accessing inclusive capital, as their opportunities for learning, gathering information and gaining access to spaces and places in the community are often restricted by their impairments or others' social attitudes (WHO, 2001). This can potentially lead to a lessening of a *sense of inclusion* in mainstream society and to a growing sense of social exclusion and isolation. In addition, previous research found that people with disabilities often found it harder to access technologies they can interact with, or to access the environments of cultural institutions and otherwise publicly available artworks (Hayhoe, 2014b; Hayhoe et al., 2015).

Through my reading, I also found that the physical nature of some disabilities or infirmities caused by old age can also lessen our access to acquiring inclusive capital (Hayhoe, 2019b). For instance, acquiring deafness and blindness later in life can make it harder to join group discussions that are an essential part of gaining information or using technology, such as smartphones. Furthermore, some people who acquire disabilities later in life often do not learn sign language or Braille or identify themselves as being disabled. Physical disabilities may also make it harder to find transport or to access cultural institutions or physical networks. Late-acquired learning disabilities can also be thought to restrict access to mainstream learning and the spaces and places of cultural institutions that people once enjoyed.

During the development of ARCHES, I felt that it was the purpose of the model developed from the Open Phase to construct a means by which to investigate the development of inclusive capital as an instrument of access. This access, I felt, would help to foster a *sense of inclusion* through engagement with, and motivate learning through, artworks. Cultural institutions, educators, scientists, engineers, artists and curators did not just need to understand this sense of inclusion intellectually and academically, it was theorised, but it was also felt that they needed to feel empathy with this *sense of inclusion*.

Practically, I also felt that the cultural institutions involved in the project also needed to understand and study ways in which they could adapt their spaces and places, both their physical and virtual environments. These institutions also needed to adapt their own behaviour to develop habits and practices that recognised a *sense of inclusion* in others. To develop this argument further, and to understand the evidence for cultural inclusion during the project, I wanted to evolve this theory by applying them to practices of developing inclusive capital from human values (Hayhoe, 2019b).

The development of participatory meetings

As stated previously, we decided that the project should be influenced by emancipatory and participatory methods, as a way of ensuring that the artworks went some way to representing the community (Henderson, 1995; Barton & Hayhoe, in press; Hayhoe & Garcia Carrisoza, 2019b). To do so, we held three open meetings with stakeholders, partners and potential artists in early 2018. Practically, as there were different issues surrounding the topic of the flooding and social inclusion involved in the project, it was decided to hold separate sessions for experts and local participants.

We held the first meeting at a university building in Bath city centre, which was designed to discuss the flooding of Bath as a topic with experts from local councils, water companies and the environment agency. This meeting focused on technical aspects of flooding, such as areas which were prone to flooding, flood defences and the history of local floods and engineered structures. Participants in the meeting included twenty-two key personnel, including local councils and river authorities, universities, arts centres, and water and sewerage companies.

We held the second meeting at the Royal National Hospital for Rheumatic Diseases (the Min), Bath city centre, and focused on local experiences of flooding and inclusion during our discussions. Eleven local participants attended the meeting, including people from a local association for the deaf, local arts institutes and associations, independent members of the community and local colleges. During this latter meeting, disabled participants also discussed their experiences of the local environment and their knowledge of the history of Bath. Although this meeting included disabled people, during this latter meeting, we decided not to collect information about participants' disabilities, as this was not felt to be necessary for the structure of the project. We were more interested in all of the participants' experiences instead.

The third of these meetings was a walk along the riverbank in Bath where the flooding occurred, to gauge the most vulnerable areas of the city and search for artefacts. All of the partners and a number of volunteer and expert stakeholders attended this walk, and we took images, some of which would be exhibited later, and discussed key, dangerous sites where the river flooding was particularly widespread. During this discussion, we noticed that there was an area of the river near the train station where historical flood levels were marked against a wall.

During the first two meetings, participants were asked what they would like to have included in the project and how they would like to see the artworks presented. These opinions were recorded through pen-and-paper notes during the session and the questionnaires, and influenced future decisions of the project. For example, where the environment was discussed during the groups, decisions were made as to where and how the eventual pieces were located.

All of these meetings provided data, which we recorded with pen and paper and by phone cameras, and preferences and suggestions for artworks and exhibition spaces were discussed in detail. For example, the meeting at the Min developed suggestions for collaborations between stakeholders and a specific interest in the "history of flooding." There was particular mention of a flood in 1968, perhaps the most devastating flood in the latter decades of the twentieth century. This community memory was a part of the life experience of many participants, and the year of the project was to be the fiftieth anniversary of the flood.

However, the first meeting of expert professionals also highlighted reservations about where the artworks could be sited along the river, with professionals from two local authorities feeling that permanent artworks would not achieve planning permission. Consequently, both meetings discussed the possibility of commissioning temporary, more portable artworks than was originally planned for.

The Axial Coding Phase

Further development of inclusive capital

During this period, I started to apply the model of inclusive capital's newly constructed stages of development. As with other forms of capital, inclusive capital was found to be acquired through life course, and a single cycle of acquiring this capital happens in five discrete and concurrent stages (Hayhoe et al., 2017; Hayhoe, 2019b).

The first stage in this cycle is connecting, bonding and forming relationships with a network of people. These groups are largely seen as a family or a group of friends, classmates or workmates, or as Yardi (2009) found, forming relationships through social media. Without forming relationships and bonding to this social or cultural network, there is no *sense of inclusion.* Thus, inclusion is premised on a social and cultural process of feeling valued in bonds and relationships.

The second stage in this cycle is learning inclusive capital through bonding, that is, a human condition to learn to develop and acquire human capital. Thus, learning inclusive capital consists of knowledge and practices that can lead to a *sense of inclusion.* In common with the writing of Smith (1776) and Marx (1867), it was felt that a part of this learning of inclusive capital is also about being seen as equally included, in order to humanise acquired skills and practices. However, and in a manner unrelated to Marx's understanding of morals, it was felt that it was during this stage when people can be said to develop a further sense, the moral sense of justice. This sense can also be described as a form of morals.

The third stage in this cycle is collecting information that points to or later leads to knowledge. This information can include finding out about our surroundings, making judgements about their worth, or planning to travel, such as directions from maps. Yardi (2009) and Bourdieu (2010) suggest such forms of cultural capital can also be acquired through the use of technology, and thus term this practice *technical capital*. In the modern era, this third stage can also mean accessing digital networks or learning, and access to these networks and this learning can develop a *sense of inclusion*. Information and technology are also a vital part of planning and designing inclusive capital and its subsequent habits and practice. During these projects, I described this stage as the raw material or the atomic level of inclusive capital.

The fourth stage in this cycle is physical or virtual access to spaces and places, such as visiting or attending cultural institutions or reading about their collections and history. In this project in particular, these spaces were community spaces such as walkways alongside the river, or temporary spaces such as exhibition spaces, festival spaces or community institutions. These institutions include places such as schools, parks, universities, museums or websites developed by organised communities.

The fifth stage in this cycle is a form of capital that weaves its way through all the others. This capital is mobility that enables navigation through spaces and places, networks, information and learning. For instance, this can include hacking and searching for information, moving between institutional environments. Consequently, mobility is an essential catalyst of the model of inclusive capital.

It was felt that the message communicated through the commissioned artworks should develop an historical understanding of the development of flooding and the dangers of living close to the river and low-lying areas – thus providing learning and information. This development was based on previous models of teaching people who had sensory or learning impairments, and was facilitated through networking and bonding.

Therefore, we commissioned the artworks as they included familiar subjects and topics through groups, that would allow all viewers and learners to relate to their topics, presentation, location and their ability to be with others. We also felt that the commissioned artworks could help the viewers explore local environments, investigating issues such as mobility and an understanding of different natural and cultural surroundings, that is, community spaces.

Applying the model of inclusive capital

As stated earlier, the first stage of applying the model of inclusive capital was the call for artists in Spring 2018, which incorporated aspects of consultation with the participatory groups. In addition to this call, we held an open evening for artists interested in submitting a proposal at 44AD, where interested artists could meet the project's stakeholders that accepted our invitation. Following this process, we decided to commission five pieces in a range of media, which engaged different senses and forms of learning and information, and which it was felt would actively engage viewers. Each of these artists and artworks is described in Appendix A.

All of the commissioned pieces represented the history of the flooding, and our decision to commission was influenced by the artists' research on flooding in Bath and their commitment to inclusive communication. As the participants requested, the artists also referred to the fiftieth anniversary of the flood of 1968. Mark Parrett, a performance artist, found local resonance from this anniversary in particular, as he came from Keynsham, which is located down-river from Bath and which was also hit by the same flooding event.

The project's website was commissioned simultaneously. As with the artworks, the website promoted the artworks and contributed to the information, learning and thus the knowledge-transfer of the project in early Spring 2018. During its development, feedback about the early page designs were provided by project participants to the developer, and suggestions about access and aesthetics led to an evolution of the website in parallel with the artworks. Initially, the website was hosted on the 44AD website. However, in Summer 2018 it was decided to buy a URL and pay for hosting, and these actions provided the project with a distinct identity that the community could relate to.

Eventually, the website developed to incorporate a description of the project as a whole, a page on the artists and their work, a calendar of events that RiV would appear in and a gallery of photos from the events and making process. In addition, the web developer also managed to create accessible pages for disabled people using internationally recognised standards by the W3C.

In Summer 2018, RiV was promoted locally at two events in Bath, events which were designed to raise awareness of the project about its aim to co-design learning with the local community. The first of the events was a stall featuring mechanically simulated flooding at Bath Festival of Nature in the city's Green Park. The Festival of Nature in particular helped to develop interest in RiV, as it was a free family festival, which was advertised in local schools and based in a park next to the River Avon. The second event was the Creative Bath Summer Party in the city's Queens Square, where the RiV partners again promoted their artworks and learning and information strategies to the local arts community.

From Autumn 2018 to early 2019, the finished artworks were exhibited and discussed at four community events in Bath, which were recommended by participants during the early meetings. The first event was European Researchers Night at the Edge Arts Centre, University of Bath. This night was designed to increase awareness of research and innovation activities at the university and showcased RiV's development to that point. During the event, we also introduced a pop-up exhibition of RiV in the art centre's Weston Studio. The researchers' night was also meant to develop public recognition of our evaluation of the project, demonstrate its impact on the daily life of the communities we worked in and encourage young people to develop their own research careers later on.

The second event was a free local arts festival called Forest of the Imagination, which began the day after European Researchers Night. In a way that was related to the Festival of Nature, Forest of the Imagination was a much larger community and family-centred festival in the centre of the city and included contemporary artworks, outdoor theatre events, sensory installations and participatory creative activities. The RiV artworks were displayed on a site running alongside the River Avon, with the exception of Mark Parrett, who performed in the nearby Kingsmead Square where other performances were taking place.

The third event was an exhibition at 44AD Art Space, Abbey Street, Bath. This arts centre was a partner, close to the Roman Baths and again followed the theme of environments near the river in Bath. This was a documentary exhibition of RiV artworks and footage of the project to date, alongside new and developed elements of some of the commissioned pieces. During the exhibition, there was also a schedule of events, including artists' talks and workshops relating to the project.

The fourth event was the documentary exhibition of the pieces by Art at the Heart, Bath Royal United Hospital. The exhibition itself covered one of the most-used stretches of corridor in the hospital, lining the walls near its reception in the main building. During this development of the project's exhibition and the reflections it generated during the Axial Phase, we formed the following hypothesis. This hypothesis tried to gauge the experiences of the artists and its effects on their personal development, in line with the project's theoretical model:

> The artworks could be developed according to the five stages of inclusive capital in order to encourage the artists to promote education, inclusion and access. Given time to reflect on this development, the

artists themselves would also consider their own practice and evolve a better understanding of inclusion.

The Selective Coding Phase

Reflections by the artists

As stated previously, restrictions voiced by the local council and river authority, which we discussed in the original stakeholder meetings, meant that developing a permanent exhibition along the river became unfeasible. In particular, the local council emphasised that artworks requiring fixtures would need planning permission that could take up to a year, extra resources and expensive legal guidance to apply for. This was beyond our budget. Similarly, the local river authority that controlled the area surrounding the river as well as the river itself counselled against the artworks being exhibited along the riverbanks.

These restrictions meant that RiV artists and participants decided it was best to make portable artworks, to exhibit in existing science and art festivals, and concentrate on the pre-planned exhibitions at 44AD and the Royal United Hospital (RUH). This meant that strategies for incorporating the environment more explicitly were not always possible, although Forest of the Imagination managed to locate artworks along a small stretch of the river during its weekend exhibition. Consequently, the interviews we carried out for the evaluation showed that there had been an emphasis on flexible design of information and learning, and less emphasis on the permanent environment of the artworks. In addition, the interviews also showed that artists networked with their audiences through their artworks, through performative practice and research.

For instance, during her interview, the commissioned installation artist Alyson Minkley described how, given the restrictions, she felt that physical accessibility needed to be flexible and negotiable. Consequently, Minkley chose to make a series of flags with historical flood levels that could be appreciated as "simply festive and fun, bringing colour & movement to draw attention to the [floods] and its purpose without having to get too close or engage too deeply."

These changes also provided an opportunity for Minkley to include elements of sensory information in her artworks beyond those she had originally considered. For instance, she told us that she found her flags managed to incorporate the acoustics of the spaces along an imagined river space when she first tried them out in the open. Minkley particularly liked this element of the artwork, as it emphasised their exhibition outdoors and allowed the flapping flags to bring-to-mind festivals and sailing. As she stated, "this [also] added an element for those without full vision."

Information, education, bonding, accessibility and artists' experience

The tensions we felt after being denied access to the spaces and places of flooding were partially offset by the information and learning experiences the artists developed as a result. In particular, these tensions meant that the artists took the opportunity to explore different elements of the history of the flooding and the dangers the community felt. This emphasised the value of personal empathy and previous roles through their pieces.

For instance, as Alyson Minkley told us, she had a relationship with the local Records Office and the city's library, and so was able to get access to flood modelling data. In addition, personal experiences of temporary disability helped her consider the mobility needs of different members of the community during her development of the flags. This was an element of her previous practice that she felt added to her overall understanding of how to communicate with people with disabilities. For instance, she told me in her interview:

> As I was recovering from a dislocated knee at the time of researching my work, I was all too well aware of physical access needs, and very short walks along the river were my first excursions.

Similarly, empathetic practices were also discussed by Marc Parrett. For instance, using the opportunity to research accessibility and flooding in the area he grew up in, Parrett also used the development of artwork to explore flooding more broadly. In particular, in his interview he explained searching for videos of international flooding on YouTube and Twitter, particularly recent flooding events. This learning experience made him more familiar with the area he was raised in and allowed him to incorporate these findings into his performance.

> Having grown up in this area the stories of the disastrous floods were often recounted, particularly on car journeys through Pensford. Although I started with a plan for my RIV piece I left space in its framework to incorporate new discoveries and developments. The piece itself kept growing even throughout its delivery during the Forest of the Imagination and related events. My only concerns for accessibility were for safety near water and traffic. As I was mostly sited away from the river bank and roads [though,] this was not an issue.

In their workshops and performances, Bridgeman and Parrett also emphasised the use of their artworks to encourage networking and bonding as part of a general learning experience about flooding. This emphasis became a deliberate element of their practice, and they both felt that this experience made them feel the whole process of creation became more accessible as a result. For example, Marc felt that the humour in his performance made the piece intrinsically more accessible, as it allowed dialogue and engagement between himself and the viewers as they had their portraits painted.

> My "sunk" piece, being an outdoor public performance could be approached by pretty much anyone of any ability. Visitors engaged with the artwork by viewing the trolley installation, the automata & water features. They could also watch the live portrait painting or sit for their portrait. Most of the "sits" took their portraits away with them. . . . One person asked me quizzically if this was a serious piece. It's an interesting point. I like dancing dangerously close to pure whimsy and my trolley of painted objects and mechanical toy dipping is a prime example of my quixotic output.

Overall experiences of access during the project

Despite our restrictions in exhibiting along the river long-term, there seemed to be increasingly positive feedback from the artists about the educational value of the project. In particular, four of the artists recorded comments by visitors who had viewed, heard or taken part in the performances, and what they had subsequently done to learn more about the city's history of floods. For instance, all of the artists taking part in the interviews described how people who had experienced the artworks had gone on to find the flood sites by the riverside, which acted as an inspiration for the events described through the various artworks. As Minkley stated:

> I have had people tell me they have been to look at the flood markings under Ha'penny Bridge & had several conversations about the phenomenal scale of water mass that the flags indicate when in position and how that would behave differently spread out in the flood conveyance system; which was rewarding to realise people understood and were as fascinated by the physical modelling of it as I am.

Similarly, three of the artists reported an increasing enjoyment of exhibiting and performing their artworks as the project progressed, finding that they also learnt a great deal through the experience of researching their pieces. All of the artists also reported that they would like to be involved in related projects in the future and would continue to consider accessibility in future pieces. For example, Parrett described how performing his artwork to a mixed audience during the exhibitions developed a sense of pleasure and wonder:

> It was a thoroughly enjoyable experience. The actual portrait painting turned out to be somewhat exhausting – more a drain on the nerves than an actual physical ordeal. The water pump worked perfectly well and the results of the "underwater colour" portraits were on the whole surprising and delightful. I'm glad I could provide a whole world of experience for visitors, so people not watching the live painting or being painted could encounter the water automata, the trolley construction and the previous paintings left to dry. . . .
>
> [In terms of access,] trusting in my process is always a big issue. I have to take risks to create work which surprises me but it does leave me feeling exposed. I have to ignore the countless internal critics and just be incredibly honest. I'm very happy that I took risks with "sunk" and I personally feel it worked on many levels. This success will undoubtedly propel me to continue making work of a similar quality and take further risks in the future.

Conclusion

The projects' educational and access aims were largely fulfilled through the planned exhibitions, execution of the performative pieces and the practice of the community when they engaged with the workshops and exhibitions. The artists reported positive feedback and that the visitors had gone out to discover further information about the flooding after engaging with their pieces. However, there were restrictions on the way exhibitions, performances and workshops could be developed. Most notably, developing more permanent access to the most relevant riverside venues, where arguably the artworks would have had a greater impact, proved impossible given the restrictions we worked within.

This was not the fault of the artists, although it is perhaps an issue that we as partners could have foreseen, as the artists could have been more actively commissioned based on these plans. However, the practicalities of the project, most notably the timing, security and legal barriers to the exhibition of the artworks, often created barriers to a more efficient use of the artworks.

Therefore, three significant lessons can be learnt from this project. Firstly, future projects with similar aims need to realise that the administration surrounding public artworks is an important consideration and possibly the greatest restriction to accessibility. Secondly, perhaps the greatest asset developed in the planning of this project was early partnerships with disabled and community partners, whose expertise was shared for the common good. For instance, the artists and expert participants often commented that they understood disabilities more as a result of this project, implying that the learning and educational aims of the artworks were a two-way street. Thirdly, what was perhaps most noticeable about the project was the communication and empathy that non-expert partners, artists, scientists and educators developed whilst producing accessible education for a STEM topic. This aim also raised awareness of a natural local issue that can help bond a community through its exploration.

Acknowledgements

River is the Venue was funded by the Public Engagement Unit at the University of Bath. We would like to acknowledge Forest of Imagination and Festival of Nature (Bath) for providing venues for exhibits and performances and the stakeholders who took part in and provided venues for the initial meetings, promotion activities, exhibitions, workshops and performances.

Appendix A

The commissioned artists included:

Ross Bennett, a fine artist, who created painted concrete columns, designed to represent samples taken from the earth using scientific machinery, thus also representing learning about spaces involved in the exhibition. The layers Bennett painted onto each of these cores represented a different sedimentary layer, laid down by the river. The pieces were designed to rest on the ground and were meant to be touched and interacted with. Being ground level height and standing up to a metre and a half tall, the pieces were also designed to be particularly accessible to people with mobility issues and children.

Edward Bettella, a musician, who created soundscapes to represent different elements of the river. The soundscapes were designed to be available at listening stations and live performances. The soundscapes became a thematic focus on four themes: 1) the flood waters and the unstoppable force of nature over hundreds of years; 2) the destruction of property and livestock, taking inspiration from the numerous accounts of people trying to protect themselves, their homes and livestock within the city; 3) the inaction of the local authorities and the population to invest in a flood prevention scheme, a story that starts in 1832; and 4) the prevention of flooding consigned to history, which the Bath Flood Prevention Scheme implemented. Each piece was designed to be no longer than one minute and thirty seconds.

Edwina Bridgeman, a fine arts educator, who proposed a series of workshops for and within the local community, engaging participants' understanding of the river and the flooding, and stimulating memories and descriptions. Thus, her project took advantage of collective community information. As part of her artwork, in the Spring of 2018 Bridgeman conducted single and repeated workshops with a local primary school close to the River Avon, a residential care centre for people with dementia next to the river, and making sessions with patients from the Royal United Hospital. These pieces subsequently formed items in display cases during the final exhibitions.

Alyson Minkley, a fine artist, who created a series of flags that ran along the river. Like Bennett, Minkley represented strata on her flags, although these strata were designed to reflect the flood levels found along the river, particularly the flood levels discussed during the walk. Minkley had also gone into greater detail, researching information about the exact height and position of the floods, making the flags represent the height of the flooding. As they flapped in the wind, the flags also made a sound and had a sense of movement, and so engaged a number of senses as well as presenting their information. The flags were also designed to look like the sails of boats, representing the water's and river's usage.

Marc Parrett, a fine artist and puppeteer, who created a mixed-media piece from flotsam and debris that was washed up by the river, based on an old pram. On the pram, Parrett also created a mechanism and pump that would take water from a tank, pump it up through a pipe and then pour it onto an A3-size sheet of paper. He then painted portraits on this sheet. During his performance, Parrett made quick self-portraits of sitters in watercolour, through which the colours ran. This piece showed the uses of water, and played with the subject in an almost comical way. For example, the water tank came with pondweed and miniature toy models of divers.

5   Grounded methodology and systematic literature reviews

Introduction

This chapter features a study of using grounded methodology to conduct a systematic review of literature, databases and online data. These are sometimes also known as topical reviews or literature surveys, as they were in ARCHES in Chapter 3. Systematic reviews are a non-traditional way of using grounded methodology, largely because systematic searches often only have a structured method of searching and thematic analysis as a default.

Having said this, although these methodologies all share the same structure, thematic analysis can be subjective, with the focus of the research being prone to biases of author's tastes. This is where grounded methodology's three stages of analysis has an advantage. By triangulating searches and analysis, this form of methodology examines data in a particular field from three different dimensions, providing a more nuanced examination of the genres of literature.

This case study was an evolution of a previous review that examined mobile learning technologies and strategies for students with disabilities, with a focus on education in the Gulf region of the Middle East (Hayhoe, 2013b). However, as discussed in Chapter 2, many studies take on a life of their own, evolve and are reproduced with different data collection strategies and topics to advance knowledge. This was the case with this systematic review, and a few years after this earlier study, I needed to understand mobile learning technologies for learners with visual impairments in all regions of the world.

What now follows is the first iteration of this study, that was presented at an international conference on learning technologies in Singapore in 2017 (Hayhoe, 2017). After this presentation, this study went through a further evolution and was subsequently prepared as a more fulsome journal article (Hayhoe, 2018b). Therefore, the study in this chapter is the middle part of this evolution that later underwent critical analysis based on feedback during and after the conference.

The chapter is broken into the six sections following this introduction: 1) the nature and aims of the study and the method of searching databases; 2) the modes of analysing the literature; 3) the open coding stage of analysis, focusing on a description of mobile devices as a case study of technological inclusion in learning environments; 4) the axial coding stage of analysis, focusing on classifications of literature on the use of mobile technology by LVI and an initial hypothesis; 5) the selective coding stage of analysis, which tests the hypothesis introduced at the end of the second stage of analysis; and 6) conclusions that were drawn from the study.

The aims, parameters and search strategies

The primary aim of the study was to discuss avenues of research in mobile learning and visual impairment to inform future pedagogical and andrological theories. The secondary aim of the study was to provide the reader with an introduction to the broader debate on the nature and role of mobile devices in the education of people who are visually impaired, and to develop a debate on the best use of technologies in mobile learning.

The planning and implementation of these aims was performed through three tasks. My first task was to set the parameters of the literature search. This is critical in such studies, and if this field is to evolve, be accurately reproduced by others and be as objective as possible, these parameters initially need to be as strict as possible. Consequently, this study became a solely English-language literature review of digital mobile devices, designed only to support or develop Learners with Visual Impairment (LVI).

This review only included learning in institutions set up for formal and informal learning, such as schools, colleges, universities, museums or other centers of cultural heritage or workplaces. The analysis focused on improving learning with mobile technologies, which was referred to as mobile learning, access to education for LVI, and the advantages of and potential problems with the use of mobile devices by and mobile learning for LVI.

As the study focused on research on visual impairment and learning, my analysis particularly focused on the influences of external factors on knowledge creation and tested an *epistemological model* as an approach to analysis (Hayhoe, 2016, 2019b). This *epistemological model* is based on the theory that the way that knowledge is created about people with visual impairment and various other disabilities has a greater effect on their lives than their physical impairments do (Hayhoe, 2015b, 2016).

When I conceived the first study, I felt it was necessary as many modern mobile technologies, such as smartphones and tablets, included accessible settings in their operating systems for users with various disabilities (Hayhoe, 2014c, 2015c). However, little theory was available at the time on their use in education, and so a growing number of overviews, updated frequently, were necessary to get an overview of the field as it grew and changed.

My second task was to develop a strategy of harvesting data through keywords or key phrases. Before starting these searches, I also grouped keywords and key phrases into two categories relating to visual impairment, mobile technologies and learning that represented the topics I planned to cover. The two categories of keyword or key phrase were called Category A and Category B, with Category A referring to different terms used for visual impairments and Category B referring to types of technology or learning.

Consequently, in each search phase, examples of Category A keywords or key phrases were to include: visual impairment, visual disabilities, blind and blindness. Similarly, examples of Category B keywords or key phrases included: e-reader, e-learning, mobile technologies, mobile learning, tablet devices and smartphones. To maintain objectivity, I had to conduct numerous searches combining each Category A keyword or key phrase with each Category B keyword or key phrase, separating each with "AND." For example, one such search was "Visual impairment AND mobile technology," with the "and" making the search exclusive to these words.

My third task was to do the searches themselves. During the searches, I used numerous research databases, institutional websites and search engines for their literature. For example, the academic databases I chose included Scopus, Web of Science, IEEE Explore, ACM and Google Scholar, as they fit the topic I was researching because I wanted to use engineering and more specialised databases, although these will need to be adjusted according to topics and subjects in different forms of study. For institutions and regular trade press searches, I used Google.

As mentioned earlier, as this is a grounded methodology study, visual impairment and mobile devices were investigated through three phases of analysis of secondary source literature. This literature included research reports and articles, previous reviews of literature, conceptual documents and reviews of technology in the trade press. The latter two categories of literature were included because there was a lack of peer-reviewed research literature in this field to provide a meaningful comparison. These methods of analysis are now discussed in greater depth as follows.

Modes of analysis

The three phases of analysis

The three-phased analysis used in this grounded methodology were carried out as follows. During the Open Coding Phase, the non-academic general and commercial literature and discussions on technology were amalgamated. From these descriptions, definitions were then reviewed to determine connections between issues, the initial nature of these connections and whether these issues could be classified and recorded in a meaningful way. This was a strategy generated during my earlier literature reviews (Hayhoe, 2013b). In terms of grounded methodology, this phase of research was analogous to starting a theatrical work, during which characters, relationships and personalities were defined and described.

Where possible, during this phase the institutional and trade literature was also read as if any prior knowledge was not acquired or theory development made; bearing in mind that I felt it was all but impossible to do this, this notion of objectivity was borne in mind and accepted as ideological, unreachable but ultimately striven for. This reading style allowed issues involving LVI, such as educational and engineering strategies, to emerge and new connections between different literatures to develop. The literature selected for this section of the research largely consisted of official documentation by English-speaking mobile technology manufacturers, institutes and non-governmental organisations (NGOs), whose role was to support LVI.

During the Axial Coding Phase, categories that arose during the Open Coding were compared to the newly searched-for academic literature. What is more, during this phase academic literature that did not appear to be initially relevant or that did not induce a pattern were put aside. In terms of grounded methodology, this process became the development of story lines, with each category I identified having its own personality, internal tensions and individual or sub-narratives. These narratives weren't yet connected, but they started to have a life and a community of their own.

As with all of these grounded methodology studies, I did not reject any documents entirely, even if they did not fit the story line I was crafting. In accordance with my methodology, I felt these outlying documents may have contained some later significance given a different context. Consequently, the sorted literature was again compared, and further concepts were analysed. From this analysis, a more targeted literature search using these newly found categories was created and a tentative first hypothesis was developed. After this, any potentially false assumptions were refuted.

After the Open and Axial Phases, the task became relatively easier. During the Selective Coding Phase, I compared the unrefined hypothesis to a more thorough analysis of academic literature against the unrefined hypothesis and tried to find strands that related categories together. In terms of grounded methodology, this was a process of bringing together all of the story lines I had individually crafted during the Axial Phase into a single, coherent story. This story was to better explain the field of knowledge created by these disparate documents.

Detailed strategies of data analysis

During the data collection and analysis in these three phases, four strategies discussed by Glaser (1998) in a later discussion of developing grounded theory were adapted for processing the literature. These four strategies included:

> *Constant comparisons.* In this study, I found that this aspect of analysis was particularly relevant in the Open Coding Phase. During this phase, I compared all of the narratives on visual impairment, technologies, cultures and education systems to identify patterns and trends of study or findings. In addition, I increasingly re-compared the literature during the following two phases to refine the hypotheses; to reject emerging patterns that didn't fit the theme of the study; to make sure that the patterns identified earlier on were not the product of literature that was limited or narrow in focus; and to retest what at first seemed irrelevant literature.
>
> *Latent patterns and core category analysis.* During the review of literature, I found that this aspect of analysis was particularly useful during the Axial Coding Phase. More particularly, my initial comparisons and development of indexes from the Open Phase underpinned categories of cultural issues that could be investigated in greater detail.
>
> In this study, these issues turned out to be the fundamental traits of curriculum development, technological design and the cultures of disability and education featured in the literature. I also found that focusing on these issues highlighted how attitudes toward visual impairment were formed, and allowed me to identify the effects of these attitudes on the LVI population and inclusive mobile technologies.
>
> *Verification.* During this study, this strategy was used during all three coding phases. It was used during the Open Coding Phase in two ways. First, I verified observable trends in the literature to categorise types of institutional and trade literature and compare any recurring themes that occurred. Second, I tried to observe individual data, such as design methodologies, which formed underpinning patterns and that could be applied to the culture of technologies and learning in the literature.

During the Axial Coding Phase, I refined these categories and patterns through further verification and by comparing theoretical literature to develop the focused hypothesis. In the Selective Coding Phase, the hypothesis was then tested using new literature by inductive observation and a more refined hypothesis emerged as a result.

Explication de text – the reading of all texts word by word in extreme detail. I found that this method of analysis was almost made for grounded methodology literature reviews, although to save time it was not applied to all the literature. As Glaser felt that literature should be included as a core component of data collection and read particularly carefully, this strategy was used in all stages, and the Open Coding Phase in particular.

For instance, I used this strategy during the analysis of trade reviews to ensure that the statistical analyses and definitions of disability used in the literature were largely comparable. However, in other cases, it was not necessary to read entire documents in such detail, as in many cases empirical and theoretical works were made up of only a limited amount of data and rarely discussed definitions of LVI.

There were also other restrictions to the use of *explication de text*. In some documents, for instance, LVI were also caught up in studies with technology users with other disabilities, so visual impairment was rarely considered as a separate topic or access need. This made making detailed findings and forming latent patterns harder, and meant I had to develop the three phases of analysis with more flexibility and reflexivity. This strategy was largely based on the experience I developed during previous grounded methodology systematic literature reviews.

What now follows is a description of the analysis process of all three phases of investigation.

The Open Coding Phase

Reviews of definitions

To begin with, when I referred to visual impairment, blindness or vision loss in education, I wanted to find out whether authors thought about LVI using an objective system. During the Open Coding Phase, I started by defining these categories in my own mind according to the international diagnosis provided by the World Health Organisation (2007, p. 1). This definition was the closest I could find to a global explanation of visual impairment, blindness and low vision – different terms used in different ways:

> "low vision" is defined as visual acuity of less than 6/18 but equal to or better than 3/60, or a corresponding visual field loss to less than 20°, in the better eye with the best possible correction. "Blindness" is defined as visual acuity of less than 3/60, or a corresponding visual field loss to less than 10°, in the better eye with the best possible correction. "Visual impairment" includes both low vision and blindness.

In addition, during this study I also decided to begin by assuming that the literature had a similar understanding of what assistive technologies referred to, and how these fell within the general category of accessible technologies. Using a method that was similar to the earlier systematic review, I defined assistive technologies according to hardware and software that supported people with disabilities. Eventually, I took this definition from an article which examined the nature of access through technologies through a lens of inclusion that was similar to the approach I wanted to take. Thus, it saw assistive technology as "an item or piece of equipment that enables individuals with disabilities to enjoy full inclusion and integration in society" (Hakobyan et al., 2013).

This definition of assistive technology raised problems, though, an issue I had discussed in previous documents. For example, traditional assistive technologies, such as hearing aids, zoom cameras and older screen readers, do not fully comply with this definition and can single out people with disabilities. As I argued in an earlier paper, these technologies are often custom made for people with disabilities and are thus exclusive and expensive (Hayhoe, 2014c).

Therefore, in this study, mainstream mobile technologies such as tablet computers were contemporaneously defined as a sub-category of accessible technologies called inclusive technologies. I felt that the inclusive nature of these technologies were their assistive features built into their mainstream operating system, something I had previously defined as "a form of mainstream technology that can be used with either no or minimal adaption by a person with a disability to enhance or increase their ability" (Hayhoe, 2014c).

Similarly, I also argued that inclusive technology had other cultural and economic benefits, especially for educators. For instance, these technologies were mass produced and marketed and thus more cost effective. They also did not single out users as disabled and made it more likely that users could integrate into mainstream classes (Hayhoe, 2015a, 2015c). Subsequently, in educational institutions, traditional assistive technologies were increasingly rare, which influenced pedagogy and andragogy.

In early reviews of mainstream teaching, I had found that teaching and learning with mobile technologies was increasingly being referred to as mobile learning, which was also sometimes called m-learning (Bachmair, 2007; Kearney et al., 2012; Kinash et al., 2012). What is more, I observed that early reviews of trade and institutional well-known commercial tablets, such as the iPad, featured heavily in research on mobile learning in mainstream settings, with mainstream technologies being adapted as learning tools (Barbour, 2012; Burden et al., 2012; Queensland Department of Education and Training, 2011; Heinrich, 2012; Kinash et al., 2012; Murray & Sloan, 2008).

Although they were not part of the current analysis, I did not start from a naïve perspective, but instead collated and fed these earlier findings into the understanding of literature in the Open Coding Phase.

Organisation and manufacturer literature

During the analysis of literature during the Open Coding Phase, I found the literature often described mobile technologies as largely accessible. These devices were also lauded by documents from specialist institutions for people with vision loss, especially for their potentially accessible features *out-of-the-box*. For instance, I found particularly positive reviews by the National Federation of the Blind (NFB, 2010, 2012) and the American Foundation of the Blind (Meddaugh, 2013) in the US, and the Royal National Institute for the Blind (RNIB, 2010; Spinks, 2012) in the UK. Although I also noted in my previous literature review that these organisations had influenced the design of these technologies, and so had previously bought into the notion of these devices as inclusive.

Despite my doubts about the total objectivity of these reviews, I also noted that some mainstream features stood out as being particularly accessible to LVI. For instance, numerous institutional reviews stated that low vision users found screen resolutions of tablets, the improved zoom facilities in these devices and their dictation software to be useful (Meddaugh, 2013; Spinks, 2012). This literature also felt that tablet and smartphone cameras were valuable for magnifying more distant objects (NFB, 2010; Meddaugh, 2013; RNIB, 2010; Spinks, 2012; Bilton, 2013). Conversely, learners who were completely blind and read Braille also found that mobile technologies could be adapted easily to make them compatible with specialist peripheral writing and reading devices (Meddaugh, 2013).

The reviews were not entirely positive, though. During analysis, I also observed that a number of studies found that these inclusive features increased processor and battery usage to the detriment of the performance of these technologies (NFB, 2010; Meddaugh, 2013). Reviewers also observed that LVI preferred smaller, more economical devices than iPads, as the cost of high-end technologies remained out of reach for many disabled people. Reviews also found that relatively cheaper devices often provided similar compatibility and did the same tasks as the more expensive ones, thus cost was not always a mark of usefulness (Spinks, 2012; Meddaugh, 2013).

My analysis of the manufacturers' own literature and reviews also showed that technology companies were actively attempting to make devices inclusive. It also appeared that these manufacturers were trying to identify functions that could potentially be of use to LVI in educational environments (Apple, 2013). In this initial phase of reading, I also noted that reviews by institutions saw the potential of mobile learning with inclusive technologies as a *disruptive technology* or a *game changer*. This disruption to current support also meant that these mobile devices could replace assistive technologies as the prominent means of support and change the practice of many LVI (RNIB, 2010; NFB, 2012). This observation was supported by manufacturers who actively worked to constantly *improve* these assistive features through consultation (Apple, 2013).

At the end of the Open Phase, I noted that the themes of constant evolution of technology, the move away from specialist devices and the consultation of user groups could provide focus in the Axial Phase. In addition, I wanted to evaluate what authors understood LVI were, what they thought their capacities were, whether there were differences in definitions on the literature on LVI and how this affected the development of mobile learning.

The Axial Coding Phase

Forming a thread of analysis

Looking back on my earlier review of mobile technologies and disability, I found that the most significant relationship was there was little research on mobile learning through the use of inclusive technologies (Hayhoe, 2013b). Similarly, during the Axial Phase I observed that much of the academic research was related as its literature over-generalised or had a very primitive understanding of visual impairment, vision loss or blindness. During this early review, I also observed that academic literature often ignored potentially valuable reviews by people with disabilities in the trade press and by national organisations. This literature also rarely referred to these institutions or their support of LVI. This was an interesting omission, as these institutions had recognised models of practice and expertise in the technological inclusion of LVI.

Research, review and conceptual documents also seemed to pose a considerable epistemological problem, as few models of mobile learning and LVI theory related any of these documents – although this in itself was a finding. More particularly, I found few global definitions or discussions of pedagogies or models of mobile learning designed with LVI in mind. This provided a problem of testable theories that could be compared, evaluated or hypothesised.

Subsequently, I made an initial classification of this literature focusing on what appeared to be three specific identifiable genres. These genres were developed according to the subject of the document, the methodological approach to LVI and their subject approach to the study. This identified three distinct categories of document: conceptual documents, documents on the design and user testing of technologies – including literature outlining proof-of-concept – and documents on evaluating existing mobile devices in-situ, including the use of these devices in mobile learning. These categories are summarised as follows.

The three categories of analysis

Conceptual Documents were the smallest category of literature I observed in this analysis. In the literature, the main epistemological trend I identified in this category were studies largely discussing mobile learning with LVI as part of a broader pedagogy of teaching all students with special needs. These issues also appeared to dominate documents even when they featured the practical needs of LVI, and the conceptualisation featured in this literature was often based on three paradigms of social science: sociological models (Hayhoe, 2015a), pedagogical models (FitzGerald et al., 2013; Fernandez-Lopez et al., 2013) and design theories (Thomson et al., 2015). By contrast, documents outlining mobile learning and LVI alone focused on reviews of the possible uses of mobile technologies as tools to support pedagogical models, rather than being pedagogical models themselves (D'Andrea & Siu, 2015; Ashraf et al., 2016).

The category **Design and User Testing of Technologies Documents** featured the design and user testing of mobile technologies and were the most common documents found in the analysis. The main epistemological trend in this literature was that the literature either followed a traditional assistive technology model, designing and reviewing custom-made hardware, or integrated technologies in mainstream mobile devices in line with the inclusive technology model.

I also found that custom-made technologies, as opposed to technologies that existed in mainstream devices, were also more likely to be used as mobile learning devices in this literature. However, all the devices I read about provided non-visual alternatives as interfaces rather than enhanced low vision. For instance, a small number of custom-made technologies were found, which were primarily designed on the principle that LVI would understand information through haptics (van der Linden et al., 2012), support traditional haptic technology through inclusive technology voice apps (Costa et al., 2015) or voice alone (Dulyan & Edmunds, 2010). These devices were designed specifically for LVI.

During analysis of this category, I also observed that documents that conformed to the inclusive technology model were designed as software platforms and situated themselves as mainstream mobile devices. Furthermore, most devices analysed or reviewed (the minority of which had an explicit educational use; van der Linden et al., 2012; Costa et al., 2015; Dulyan & Edmunds, 2010; Pesek et al., 2015; Santoro et al., 2007) were also integrated into mainstream mobile devices and primarily relied on Audible interfaces (Hakobyan et al., 2013; Long et al., 2016; Guerrero et al., 2012; Masudul Haque et al., 2015; Martinez-Perez et al., 2013). Fewer documents still discussed the use of existing and native voice apps for making mobile devices more generally accessible for LVI (Rafael et al., 2013; Azenkot & Lee, 2013).

Conversely, I found that **Mobile Learning In-Situ Documents** were less numerous than documents featuring the design of mobile devices, yet significantly more than the Conceptual Documents category. The main epistemological trend in this literature was the use of mobile technologies as a tool for providing support for students in mainstream learning or working environments (Istenic Starcic & Bagon, 2014; Pavlik, 2017; Hayhoe et al., 2015; Kaldenberg & Smallfield, 2016; Hayhoe et al., 2017; Pal & Lakshmanan, 2015; Mason, 2014), independent learning (Rogers & Draffan, 2016; Piper et al., 2016) or unique learning settings (Wong & Tan, 2012; Hussein et al., 2015; Campana & Ouimet, 2015). I concluded therefore that this category was more likely to conform to a model of inclusive technology.

I also observed that this category of documents, although numerically fewer, were less likely to feature adult learners, although this adult literature was more likely to feature support for learning in non-traditional learning or working environments. Conversely, literature featuring mobile learning by children traditionally focused almost exclusively on classroom environments. Moreover, I found that documents in this category were more likely to focus on integrated media and communication technologies as a tool of mainstreaming students with special needs (Istenic Starcic & Bagon, 2014; Pavlik, 2017; Hayhoe et al., 2015).

After collating the findings from the Axial Phase, I made two focused findings that could be adapted as themes: 1) there was an imbalance in the literature on articificially testing apps rather than evaluating mobile technologies as systems of learning or discussing their advantages in educational environments; and 2) although efforts were made to strategise and develop a role for mobile technologies in the teaching of LVI, there were no joined-up strategies in the literature on the use of technologies in individual learning contexts. I then expressed these findings as the following unrefined hypothesis:

> Mobile technologies designed to support mobile learning do not align with those studies of the use of mobile technologies in learning environments with LVI, therefore no single epistemological trend has emerged to guide researchers and writers from different fields.

The Selective Coding Phase

Testing the unrefined hypothesis

To test this hypothesis, I analysed literature referring only to mobile learning and LVI, and specifically referred to documents focusing on LVI as a single group and not visual impairment as a subset of special needs. This provided a specific focus that was analysed through *explication de text*, allowing a theoretically more accurate analysis of data. This re-analysis of the literature appeared to show that sampling the evaluations of designs rarely sampled LVI who tested new technologies. Furthermore, this literature also seemed to account for most of the population who had residual vision, but developed technologies for LVI with no sight and no experience of vision.

For example, seeming to ignore the literature by institutions working with LVI (NFB, 2010, 2012; Meddaugh, 2013; RNIB, 2010; Spinks, 2012), literature in the Design and User Testing of Technologies Documents category often designed customised apps and tested on the assumption that blind people would not want interfaces with any visual references (van der Linden et al., 2012; Costa et al., 2015; Dulyan & Edmunds, 2010; Pesek et al., 2015). This contrasted with the documents in the Conceptual Documents category, which mainly featured LVI and general learners and mentioned perceptual need less (D'Andrea & Siu, 2015; Ashraf et al., 2016).

During this re-analysis, I also observed that there was a significant difference in the approach to evaluations of technologies by literature in the Mobile Learning In-Situ Documents and Design and User Testing of Technologies Documents categories. For instance, documents in the former category tended to explore existing mobile settings and apps to support LVI in general learning and training environments (Kaldenberg & Smallfield,

2016; Hayhoe et al., 2017; Pal & Lakshmanan, 2015; Mason, 2014; Rogers & Draffan, 2016; Piper et al., 2016; Wong & Tan, 2012; Hussein et al., 2015; Campana & Ouimet, 2015). In contrast, the latter category tended to focus on mobile technologies as tools of individual learning tasks through customised technologies (van der Linden et al., 2012; Costa et al., 2015; Dulyan & Edmunds, 2010; Pesek et. al., 2015; Santoro et al., 2007). Therefore, I concluded that Design and User Testing of Technologies Documents literature tended to support a more traditional model of assistive technology, and LVI were often encouraged to use separate technologies (Hayhoe, 2014a).

This disparity in the research and theorisation of these three categories supported the aspects of the hypothesis that "no single epistemological trend has emerged to guide researchers and writers from different fields." This being said, I also found evidence that this hypothesis needs further refinement. In particular, there was a partial trend in all of the categories in comparison to my previous systematic review that the notion of assistive technology was generally moving towards a model of inclusion in educational environments.

For instance, the Mobile Learning In-Situ Documents and Conceptual Documents categories featured literature on mobile devices adapted from mainstream technologies used in mainstream environments (Kaldenberg & Smallfield, 2016; Hayhoe et al., 2017; Pal & Lakshmanan, 2015; Mason, 2014; Rogers & Draffan, 2016; Piper et al., 2016). Similarly, I observed that the literature in the Design and User Testing of Technologies Documents category placed emphasis on the design of software and apps that could be used with sighted peers (van der Linden et al., 2012; Costa et al., 2015; Dulyan & Edmunds, 2010; Pesek et al., 2015; Santoro et al., 2007). Therefore, it appeared that there was a general social will to support an inclusive model of education, but methodologies were still too young and immature to be able to develop a coherent form of technology that could fit this aim.

Conclusion

The findings in all three phases of analysis led me to conclude that although there was still a relatively small literature on LVI and mobile learning, the volume of documents was increasing rapidly. Consequently, it was possible to identify distinct bodies of literature that had their own way of creating, theorising or using technology to support LVI. However, despite this new body of literature, there was still little cohesion or a focused philosophy of research and conceptualisation that bound these studies together. Engineers writing on the design and testing of new devices, in particular, appeared to be out of step with the needs of most LVI, favouring traditional assistive models instead.

Therefore, I felt that until all researchers in this field could take a step back and communicate with each other about the needs of LVI, and more importantly understand LVI as a learning community, it would take longer to develop technologies and mobile learning strategies that could support them to their greatest benefit.

6 Conclusion

To summarise, grounded methodology was developed from grounded theory, which itself began as a highly structured methodology of social science and was designed to study previously under-researched topics. Through research practice, both grounded theory and grounded methodology gather largely qualitative data, although previously gathered statistics and analysed data can also be collected to support this analysis.

However, grounded methodology was developed as a different methodology from a desire to move away from grounded theory's core philosophy and what was felt to be its impractical complexity. Grounded theory was originally based on inductive logic, but grounded methodology moved away from this form of logic to become a largely deductive form of study. The resulting social and cultural style of analysis accepted its own biases and encouraged hypotheses and questioning formation throughout investigation.

The constant hypothecation and questioning created during grounded methodology studies were tested and compared throughout grounded methodology's research practice. Through this mode of analysis, grounded methodology studies developed a narrative which can be described as a form of thick description.

This form of analysis also leads to another significant difference between grounded theory and grounded methodology: grounded theory codes data in a structured way, whereas grounded methodology creates a discourse and then a narrative to explain phenomena or a topic of study. At the core of this grounded methodology narrative are the relationships between and within categories. Consequently, in subsequent research studies, I found that grounded methodology had a number of advantages in the contexts of their individual settings, and thus my studies became more focused, flexible, creative and practical.

This summary of grounded methodology's process of analysing and then narrating communities, societies and cultures leads me back to the hypothesis I introduced at the beginning of this book. This hypothesis is:

Grounded methodology focuses on the theory that relationships can most often provide the richest understanding of our human societies and cultures. These relationships are, most importantly, the relationships formed between people, communities, institutions, epistemologies (that is, families or types of knowledge) or forms of learning. However, in addition to "real world" relationships, grounded methodology also focuses on relationships among data, categories of data and the underlying relationships that underpin similarities or differences between these data and categories.

As a universal statement, it would be impossible to prove this hypothesis, although this is not the core of the philosophy of grounded methodology, which believes that each context has its own internal social and cultural logic. However, it is arguable that from the evidence of the three case studies featured in this book, this hypothesis has enough validity to make grounded methodology studies meaningful and their outcomes useful. At the end of the day, in education at least, this is the most we can hope to achieve.

For instance, during the ARCHES project, the relationships between the participants led to a rich, thick discourse. This discourse helped the participants to develop their own community of learning, knowledge and practice that led to new forms of technology and provided a starting point for the development of further inclusive technologies. Importantly, although these technologies were focused on museums, there were underpinning concepts that could be hypothesised during future projects. Thus, a new direction for data collection and analysis was also created.

Similarly, the model of inclusive capital used as a focus for RiV, which itself was developed through ARCHES, also provided a direction for developing educational practice that was related to the theme of flooding. This model also underpinned the relationships between the participants in the project, which came from the different stakeholders of professionals, artists and the public, who formed a learning community in the city of Bath. The results of these relationships were a coherent narrative that led to disparate and inclusive artworks, which saw flooding as a multi-modal phenomenon. Thus, the exhibition of these artworks enriched the learning process and the experiences of the artists who created these artworks.

Finally, the systematic literature review featured in Chapter 5 included the relationships within and between genres and categories of literature, and each of these genres featured a different mode of epistemology and mode of study. Each of these genres had its own internal logical relationships and highlighted its relationships to other categories, even though some of these relationships appeared to be distant. Thus, again these relationships and the categories that joined them together became the basis of a coherent narrative, one that told the story of the study of the development and use of inclusive technologies.

Thus, I finish this exposition of grounded methodology by arguing that the need for this methodology is a subjective one. It is a need that fits the needs of myself and other researchers I have worked with on grounded methodology projects in specific unique contexts where little theory or prior work exists. In this way, grounded methodology is not the answer to all situations, and like grounded theory it is a specialist methodology that is only useful in exceptional contexts. It is also not the answer to all of science or social sciences' problems; it is merely a step along a path that we ourselves create.

References

Adorno, T., Frenkel-Brenswik, E., Levinson, D. J., & Sanford, R. N. (2019). *The authoritarian personality*. New York: Verso Books.

Apple. (2013). *Accessibility*. Downloaded from www.apple.com/accessibility/ (accessed March 2020).

Argyropoulos, V. S., & Kanari, C. (2015). Re-imagining the museum through "touch": Reflections of individuals with visual disability on their experience of museum-visiting in Greece. *Alter*, 9(2), 130–143.

Ashraf, M., Hasan, N., Lewis, L., & Hasan, R. (2016). A systematic literature review of the application of information communication technology for visually impaired people. *International Journal of Disability and Management*, 11(6).

Azenkot, S., & Lee, N. B. (2013). Exploring the use of speech input by blind people on mobile devices. *Proceedings of ASSETS 2013–15th international ACM SIGACCESS conference on computers and accessibility*. New York: ACM.

Bachmair, B. (2007). M-learning and media use in everyday life: Towards a research agenda. *Occasional Papers in Work Based Learning*, 1, 105–152.

Barbour, M. K. (2012). Teachers perceptions of iPads in the classroom. *MACUL Journal*, 32(4), 25–26.

Barton, J., & Hayhoe, S. (in press). *Emancipatory and participatory research for emerging educational researchers*. Abbingdon: Routledge.

BERA. (2018). *Ethical guidelines for ethical research* (4th ed.). London: British Educational Research Association.

Bilton, N. (2013, September 29th). Disruptions: Visually impaired turn to smartphones to see their world. *New York Times*. Downloaded from https://bits.blogs.nytimes.com/2013/09/29/disruptions-guided-by-touch-screens-blind-turn-to-smartphones-for-sight/ (accessed March 2020).

Bourdieu, P. (2010). *Distinction*. London: Routledge Classics.

Burden, K., Hopkins, P., Male, T., Martin, S., & Trala, C. (2012). *iPad Scotland evaluation*. Hull, Humberside: University of Hull.

Campana, L. V., & Ouimet, D. A. (2015). iStimulation: Apple iPad use with children who are visually impaired, including those with multiple disabilities. *Journal of Visual Impairment & Blindness*, 109(1), 67–72.

Charmaz K., (2006). Constructing Grounded Theory: A practical guide through qualitative analysis. Thousand Oaks, CA: Sage.

Costa, L. C. P., Correa, A. G. D., Dalmon, D. L., Zuffo, M. K., & Lopes, R. D. (2015). Accessible educational digital book on tablets for people with visual impairment. *IEEE Transactions on Consumer Electronics*, 61(3), 271–278.

D'Andrea, F. M., & Siu, Y.-T. (2015). Students with visual impairments: Considerations and effective practices for technology use. In Edyburn, D. L. (Ed.). *Efficacy of assistive technology interventions*. London: Emerald Insight.

Deflem, M. (2013). The structural transformation of sociology. *Society*, 50(2), 156–166.

Dulyan, A., & Edmunds, E. (2010). AUXie: Initial evaluation of a blind accessible virtual museum tour. *In OZCHI '10: Proceedings of the 22nd conference of the computer human interaction special interest group of Australia on computer human interaction*. New York: ACM.

European Union. (2020). *Technical innovations help overcome access barriers to cultural spaces*. Downloaded from https://cordis.europa.eu/article/id/413505-technical-innovations-help-overcome-access-barriers-to-cultural-spaces (accessed March 2020).

Evans-Pritchard, E. E. (1962). *Social anthropology and other essays*. New York: The Free Press.

Fernandez,-Lopez, A., Rodriguez-Fortiz, M., Rodriguez-Almendos, M. L., & Martinez-Segura, M. (2013). Mobile learning technology based on iOS devices to support students with special education needs. *Computers & Education*, 61(1), 77–90.

Feyerabend, P. (1993). *Against method*. New York: Verso.

FitzGerald, E., Ferguson, R., Adams, A., Gaved, M., Mor, Y., & Thomas, R. (2013). Augmented reality and mobile learning: The state of the art. *International Journal of Mobile and Blended Learning*, 5(4), 43–58.

Geertz, C. (1989). *Works and lives: The anthropologist as author*. Palo Alto, CA: Stanford University Press.

Glaser, B. G. (1998). *Doing grounded theory: Issues and discussions*. Mill Valley, CA: The Sociology Press.

Glaser, B. G. (2001). *The grounded theory perspective: Conceptualization contrasted with description*. Mill Valley, CA: Sociology Press.

Glaser, B. G., & Strauss, A. L. (1965). *An awareness of dying*. Chicago, IL: Aldine Publishing Company.

Glaser, B. G., & Strauss, A. L. (1967). *The discovery of grounded theory: Strategies for qualitative research*. Chicago, IL: Aldine Publishing Company.

Goffman, E. (1959). *The presentation of self in everyday life*. New York: Doubleday.

Guerrero, L. A., Vasquez, F., & Ochoa, S. F. (2012). An indoor navigation system for the visually impaired. *Sensors*, 12(6), 8236–8258.

Hakobyan, L., Lumsden, J., O'Sullivan, D., & Bartlett, H. (2013). Mobile assistive technologies for the visually impaired. *Survey of Ophthalmology*, 58(6), https://doi.org/10.1016/j.survophthal.2012.10.004

Hall, T., & Robertson, I. (2001). Public art and urban regeneration: Advocacy, claims and critical debates. *Landscape Research*, 26(1), 5–26.

Hayhoe, S. (2012). *Grounded theory and disability studies: Researching legacies of blindness*. Amherst, NY: Cambria Press.

Hayhoe, S. (2013a). A practice report of students from a school for the blind leading groups of younger mainstream students in visiting a museum and making multi-modal artworks. *Journal of Blindness Innovation & Research*, 3(2), 4. http://doi.org/10.5241/2F3-43

Hayhoe, S. (2013b). A review of the literature on the use of mobile tablet computing as inclusive devises for students with disabilities. *Proceedings of the current trends in information technology 2013 conference*. NJ: IEEE.

Hayhoe, S. (2014a). A philosophy of inclusive technology for people with special needs, and its application in a course using mobile computing devices for undergraduates at the London School of Economics, UK. *Proceedings of EDULEARN14: Education and new learning technologies*. Valencia, Spain: IATED.

Hayhoe, S. (2014b). An enquiry into passive and active exclusion from sensory aesthetics in museums and on the Web: Two case studies of final year students at California School for the Blind studying art works through galleries and on the web. *British Journal of Visual Impairment*, 32(1), 44–58.

Hayhoe, S. (2014c). The need for inclusive accessible technologies for students with disabilities and learning difficulties. In Burke, L. (Ed.). *Learning in a digitalized age: Plugged in, turned on, totally engaged?* Melton: John Catt Educational Publishing, pp. 257–274.

Hayhoe, S. (2015a). A pedagogical evaluation of accessible settings in Google's Android and Apple's iOS mobile operating systems and native apps using the SAMR model of educational technology and an educational model of technical capital. *INTED2015 proceedings, 9th international technology, education and development conference*. Valencia, Spain: IATED.

Hayhoe, S. (2015b). *Philosophy as disability & exclusion: The development of theories on blindness, touch and the arts in England, 1688–2010*. Charlotte, NC: IAP.

Hayhoe, S. (2015c). Utilising mobile technologies for students with disabilities. In Robertson, A. with Jones-Parry, R. (Eds.). *Commonwealth education partnerships: 2015/16*. Cambridge: Commonwealth Secretariat & Nexus Strategic Partnerships.

Hayhoe, S. (2016). The epistemological model of disability, and its role in understanding passive exclusion in Eighteenth & Nineteenth Century Protestant educational asylums. *International Journal of Christianity and Education*, 20(1), 49–66.

Hayhoe, S. (2017). Mobile devices, M-Learning & Learners with visual impairment: Epistemological trends analysed through a grounded methodology literature review. Paper presented at *International conference of education and e-Learning*. Singapore, Singapore.

Hayhoe, S. (2018). Epistemological trends in the literature on mobile devices, mobile learning, and learners with visual impairments. *Optometry and Vision Science*, 95(9), 889–897. https://doi.org/10.1097/OPX.0000000000001279

Hayhoe, S. (2019a). Inclusive technical capital in the twenty-first century. In Halder, S. & Argyropoulos, V. (Eds.). *Inclusion, equity and access for individuals with disabilities*. Singapore: Palgrave Macmillan, pp. 223–241. https://doi.org/10.1007/978-981-13-5962-0_11

Hayhoe, S. (2019b). *Cultural heritage, ageing, disability and identity: Practice, and the development of inclusive capital* (Routledge Studies in Heritage). Abbingdon, Oxfordshire: Routledge.

Hayhoe, S., Cohen, R., & Garcia Carrizosa, H. (2019). Locke and Hume's philosophical theory of color is investigated through a case study of Esref Armagan, an artist born blind. *Journal of Blindness Innovation and Research*, 9(1). http://doi.org/10.5241/9-149. Downloaded from https://nfb.org/images/nfb/publications/jbir/jbir19/jbir090103.html.

Hayhoe, S., & Garcia Carrisoza, H. (2019a). *Accessible Resources for Cultural Heritage EcoSystems (ARCHES) deliverable 6.5: Evaluation of pilot exercises* (4th ed.). Brussels: European Commission.

Hayhoe, S., & Garcia Carrisoza, H. (2019b). *Accessible Resources for Cultural Heritage EcoSystems (ARCHES) deliverables 2.4: Recommendations, guidelines & policy briefing* (4th ed.). Brussels: European Commission.

Hayhoe, S., Garcia Carrisoza, H., Rix, J., Sheehy, K., & Seale, J. (2019). A survey of networked and Wi-Fi enabled practices to support disabled learners in museums. In *2019 15th IEEE international conference on wireless and mobile computing, networking and communications (WiMob)* (vol. 15, pp. 197–202). [8923129]. New York: IEEE. https://doi.org/10.1109/WiMOB.2019.8923129.

Hayhoe, S., Pena-Sanchez, N., & Bentley, K. (2017). Evaluation of a collaborative photography workshop using the iPad 2 as an accessible technology for participants who are blind, visually impaired and sighted working collaboratively. *Proceedings of the 2017 14th IEEE annual consumer communications & networking conference*. NJ: IEEE.

Hayhoe, S., Roger, K., Eldritch-Boersen, S., & Kelland, L. (2015). Developing inclusive technical capital beyond the Disabled Students' Allowance in England. *Social Inclusion*, 3(6), 29–41.

Hayhoe, S., Tonin, C., & Lunardi, G. (2017, October). A model of inclusive capital for analysis of non-economic human capital. *Poster session presented at Decent Work, Equity and Inclusion*. Padova, Italy.

Heinrich, P. (2012). *The iPad as a tool for education: A study of the introduction of iPads at Longfield Academy, Kent*. Nottingham: NAACE: The ICT Association.

Henderson, D. J. (1995). Consciousness raising in participatory research: Method and methodology for emancipatory nursing inquiry. *Advances in Nursing Science*, 17(3), 58–69.

Hussein, A. H., AlHaisoni, M. M., Mohammed, A. A. B., & Fakrudeen, M. (2015). M-Learning for blind students using touch screen mobile apps case study-special education in Hail. *International Journal of Computer Science and Information Security*, 13(12), 82–88.

Istenic Starcic, A., & Bagon, S. (2014). ICT-supported learning for inclusion of people with special needs: Review of seven educational technology journals, 1970–2011. *British Journal of Educational Technology*, 45(2), 202–230.

Jeřábek, H. (2001). Paul Lazarsfeld – The founder of modern empirical sociology: A research biography. *International Journal of Public Opinion Research*, 13, 229–244.

Johnson, N. (1995). Cast in stone: Monuments, geography, and nationalism. *Environment and Planning D – Society and Space*, 13(1), 51–65.

Kaldenberg, J., & Smallfield, S. (2016). Using the iPad to facilitate daily activity among older adults with low vision: A pilot study. *American Journal of Occupational Therapy*, 70(4_Supplement_1), 7011520292p1–7011520292p1.

Kearney, M., Schuck, S., Burden, K., & Aubusson, P. (2012). Viewing mobile learning from a pedagogical perspective. *Research in Learning and Technology*, 20, 1–17.

Kinash, S., Brand, J., & Mathew, T. (2012). AJET 28 Challenging mobile learning discourse through research: Student perceptions of Blackboard Mobile Learn and iPads. *Australian Journal of Educational Technology*, 28(4), 639–655.

Kuhn, T. S., (1962). *The Structure of Scientific Revolution*. Chicago, IL: Chicago University Press.

Kuhn, T. S. (1996). *The structure of scientific revolution* (3rd ed.). Chicago, IL: Chicago University Press.

Lakatos, I. (1970). *Falsification and scientific research programmes: Criticism and the growth of scientific knowledge*, eds. I. Lakatos & A. Musgrave. Cambridge: Cambridge University Press.

Lakatos, I. (2015). *Proofs and refutations: The logic of mathematical discovery*. Cambridge: Cambridge University Press.

Levinson, S. (2018). *Written in stone: Public monuments in changing societies*. Durham, NC: Duke University Press.

Locke, J. (2001). *An essay concerning human understanding*. London: Everyman Library/J.M. Dent.

Long, S. K., Karpinsky, N. D., Doner, H., & Still, J. D. (2016). Using a mobile application to help visually impaired individuals explore the outdoors. *Advances in design for inclusion – Proceedings of the 2016 AHFE conference*. New York: Springer.

Martinez-Perez, B., de-la Torre-Diez, I., & Loez-Cononado, M. (2013). Mobile health applications for the most prevalent conditions by the World Health Organization: Review and analysis. *Journal of Medical Internet Research*, 15(6). Downloaded from www.jmir.org/2013/6/e120/

Marx, K. (1867). (1986 edition). *Capital – A critique of political economy: The process of production of capital* (vol. 1). Moscow, Russia: Progress Publishers.

Mason, T. (2014). Transforming teaching: Implementing mobile technology learning strategies in serving students with visual impairments. *Unpublished doctoral dissertation*, Texas Tech University, US.

Masudul Haque, A. M., Nahar, F., & Ahmed, N. (2015). Ifreephony: A touchscreen based user interface for people with visual impairment. *Proceedings of 10th global engineering, science and technology conference*. Dhaka, Bangladesh: BIAM Foundation.

Meddaugh, J. J. (2013). 2012: A technology year in review. *AccessWorld*, 14, 2 (accessed 3rd March 2020).

Mills, J., Bonner, A., & Francis, K. (2006). The development of constructivist grounded theory. *International Journal of Qualitative Methods*, 5(1), 25–35.

Mitchell, W. J. (1990). The violence of public art: "Do the right thing." *Critical Inquiry*, 16(4), 880– 899.

Motterlini, M. (1999). *For and against method*. Chicago, IL: Chicago University Press.

Murray, C., & Sloan, J. (2008). *iPod Touch research report*. Victoria: Department of Education and Early Childhood Development.

Neumüller, M., & Reichinger, A. (2013, April). From stereoscopy to tactile photography. *PhotoResearcher*, 19, 59–63.

NFB. (2010). *National federation of the blind commends apple for including VoiceOver on iPad*. Downloaded from https://nfb.org/node/1083 (accessed December 2010).

NFB. (2012). *The new iPad*. Downloaded from https://nfb.org/blog/atblog/newipad. (accessed October 2012).

Pal, J., & Lakshmanan, M. (2015). Mobile devices and weak ties: A study of vision impairments and workplace access in Bangalore. *Disability and Rehabilitation: Assistive Technology*, 10(4), 323–331.

Parsons, T., Shils, E. A., & Smelser, N. J. (Eds.). (1965). *Toward a general theory of action: Theoretical foundations for the social sciences*. Piscataway, NJ: Transaction Publishers.

Pavlik, J. V. (2017). Experiential media and disabilities in education: Enabling learning through immersive, interactive, customizable, and multi-sensorial digital platforms. *Ubiquitous Learning: An International Journal*, 10(1), 15–22.

Pesek, M., Kuhl, D., Baloh, M., & Marolt, M. (2015). ZaznajSpoznaj – A modifiable platform for accessibility and inclusion of visually-impaired elementary school children. *The proceedings of international conference on informatics in schools: Situation, evolution and perspectives – ISSEP 2015*. Ljubljana, Slovenia: University of Ljubljana.

Piper, A. M., Brewer, R., & Cornejo, R. (2016). Technology learning and use among older adults with late-life vision impairments. *Universal Access in the Information Society*, 15(1), 1–13.

Popper, K. (1934). *Logik der Forschung*. Wien: J. Springer.

Popper, K. (1959). *The logic of scientific discovery*. London: Hutchinson & Co.

Popper, K. (1963). *Conjectures and refutations: The growth of scientific knowledge*. London: Routledge.

Popper, K. (1999). *The open society and its enemies: Volume 1 the spell of Plato* (5th ed.). London: Routledge.

Queensland Department of Education and Training. (2011). *iPad Trial: Is the iPad suitable as a learning tool in schools?* Queensland, Australia: Government of Queensland.

Rafael, I., Luís Duarte, L., Carriço, L., & Guerreiro, T. (2013). Towards ubiquitous awareness tools for blind people. *BCSHCI '13 – Proceedings of the 27th international BCS human computer interaction conference*. New York: ACM.

Rix, J. (2007). Labels of opportunity – A response to carson and rowley, ethical space. *The International Journal of Communication Ethics*, 4(3), 25–28.

Rix, J., Garcia Carrisoza, H., Seale, J., Sheehy, K., & Hayhoe, S. (2019). The while of participation: A systematic review of participatory research involving people with sensory impairments and/or intellectual impairments. *Disability & Society*, 1–27. https://doi.org/10.1080/09687599.2019.1669431.

RNIB. (2010). *Could the iPad start a revolution in access for blind and partially sighted consumers?* Downloaded from www.rnib.org.uk/aboutus/mediacentre/

mediareleases/mediareleases2010/Pages/mediarelease28May2010.aspx (accessed June 2010).

Rogers, N., & Draffan, E. A. (2016, April). Evaluating the mobile web accessibility of electronic text for print impaired people in higher education. In *Proceedings of the 13th web for all conference.* ACM, p. 26.

Santoro, C., Paternò, F., Ricci, G., & Leporini, B. (2007). A multimodal mobile museum guide for all. *Proceedings of IEEE 2007 workshop HCI mobile guides.* NJ: IEEE.

Seale, J., Garcia-Carrisoza, H., Rix, J., Sheehy, K., & Hayhoe, S. (2018). A proposal for a unified framework for the design of technologies for people with learning difficulties. *Technology and Disability,* 30(2), 25–40. https://doi.org/10.3233/TAD-180193.

Sheehy, K., Ferguson, R., & Clough, G. (2014). *Augmented education: Bringing real and virtual learning together* (Digital Education and Learning). Basingstoke: Palgrave Macmillan.

Sheehy, K., Garcia-Carrizosa, H., Rix, J., Seale, J., & Hayhoe, S. (2019). Inclusive museums and augmented reality: Affordances, participation, ethics, and fun. *International Journal of the Inclusive Museum,* 12(4), 67–85. https://doi.org/10.18848/1835-2014/CGP/v12i04/67-85.

Smith, A. (1776). *Wealth of nations* (2005 ed.). Chicago, IL: University of Chicago Press.

Smith, H. J., Ginley, B., & Goodwin, H. (2013). Beyond compliance? Museums, disability and the law. In Sandell, R., & Nightingale, E. (Eds.). *Museums, equality and social justice.* Abbingdon: Routledge, pp. 83–95.

Spence, C. (2010). Cross modal attention. *Scholarpedia,* 5(5), 6309.

Spinks, R. (2012). *200 hours with the new iPad.* Downloaded from www.rnib.org.uk/livingwithsightloss/computersphones/updates/ (accessed December 2012).

Strauss, A., & Corbin, J. (1990). *Basics of qualitative research* (vol. 15). Newbury Park, CA: Sage.

Thomson, R., Fichten, C. S., Havel, A., Budd, J., & Asuncion, J. (2015). Blending universal design, e-learning, and information and communication technologies. In *Universal design in higher education: From principles to practice.* Cambridge, MA: Harvard University Press, pp. 275–284.

van der Linden, J., Braun, T., Rogers, Y., Oshodi, M., Spiers, A., McGoran, D., et al. (2012). Haptic lotus: A theatre experience for blind and sighted audiences. In *Proceedings of the 2012 ACM annual conference: Extended abstracts on human factors in computing systems (CHI EA '12).* Austin, TX.

WHO. (2001). *International classification of functioning, disability and health: ICF.* Geneva, Switzerland: World Health Organisation.

Wong, M. E., & Tan, S. S. K. (2012). Teaching the benefits of smart phone technology to blind consumers: Exploring the potential of the iPhone. *Journal of Visual Impairment and Blindness,* 106, 10. Downloaded from www.afb.org/afbpress/pubjvib.asp?DocID=jvib0610toc.

World Health Organisation. (2007). *Global initiative for the elimination of avoidable blindness: Action plan 2006–2011.* Geneva: World Health Organisation.

Yardi, S. (2009). Social learning and technical capital on the social web. *ACM Crossroads*, 16(2), 9–11.

Yardi, S. (2010, February). A theory of technical capital. *Paper presented at the TMSP workshop, georgia institute of technology.* Georgia, US. Downloaded from http://tmsp.umd.edu/position%20papers/Yardi-SocialMediatingTech.pdf (accessed March 2020).

Index

For Product Safety Concerns and Information please contact our EU
representative GPSR@taylorandfrancis.com
Taylor & Francis Verlag GmbH, Kaufingerstraße 24, 80331 München, Germany

www.ingramcontent.com/pod-product-compliance
Ingram Content Group UK Ltd.
Pitfield, Milton Keynes, MK11 3LW, UK
UKHW021259130625
459435UK00020B/10